proc

DAUGHTER OF REVOLUTION

DAUGHTER OF REVOLUTION
A Russian girlhood remembered

❖❖❖

VERA BROIDO

Constable · London

First published in Great Britain 1998 by Constable and Company Limited
3 The Lanchesters, 162 Fulham Palace Road, London W6 9ER
Copyright © Vera Broido 1998
ISBN 0 09 479110 4
The right of Vera Broido to be identified as author of this work has been
asserted by her in accordance with the Copyright, Designs and Patents Act
1988
Set in Monotype Garamond 12pt by Servis Filmsetting Ltd, Manchester·
Printed in Great Britain by St Edmundsbury Press, Bury St Edmunds, Suffolk

A CIP catalogue record for this book is available from the British Library

To my family, past and present

Illustrations

[7]

My father with Frederic Voigt
The author as a Red Scout in Petrograd, 1919
My brother Danya in Berlin, 1923
My mother, Eva, 1926 or 1927
Alexandra Exter in Paris, 1920
Raoul Hausmann as dancer, 1929
The author with Raoul Hausmann around 1929
Ibiza in the early 1930s by Raoul Hausmann
The author in England, 1937

I

In my childhood there were no palaces or mansions, no country estates with parks and avenues, no titled relatives or illustrious ancestors – I did not belong to that world. But for all that, my childhood did not lack romance. My parents, Mark and Eva Broido, were revolutionaries, and their freedom, even their lives, were in constant danger from the secret police. Revolutionaries in tsarist Russia were always on the run, much of the time in hiding. Often enough they were caught, imprisoned, exiled to Siberia (with or without a trial), sent into *katorga* (hard labour), or even hanged.

I was brought up to love and admire the heroes of the revolutionary movement. First came the Decembrists, that group of intrepid army officers who in December 1825 dared to interrupt a grand military parade in St Petersburg with demands for constitutional and social reform. Many of these young men belonged to the oldest families of the Russian nobility. They had been through the Napoleonic Wars and followed their emperor on his European journey, to Paris, London, Vienna. They had returned full of new ideas and were eager to see them implemented. They paid dearly for their boldness. Five of them went to the gallows and the rest were sent to the gold mines in far Siberia.

I was deeply moved by Pushkin's letter-poem to the Decembrists. I wept over Nikolay Nekrasov's epic poem *Russian Women*, in which he describes the heroism and sufferings of the young wives who followed their husbands to Siberia. The two young wives in question, Princess Volkonskaya and Countess Trubetskaya, were pampered society beauties, quite unprepared for the ordeal that awaited them.

The Decembrists were few in number and were easily silenced. But neither the introduction of a secret police nor stricter censorship and control of foreign travel could prevent further developments. The Decembrists had opened a window on to the world. Both the Russian intelligentsia and the Russian revolutionary movement were born in the aftermath of their revolt. The intelligentsia inherited their sense of honour. Not every individual lived up to that high ideal, but the ideal itself survived. Though the intelligentsia was by no means monolithic – it included westernisers and Slavophiles, religious believers and atheists – all shared the same values of integrity and intellectual probity.

The revolutionary movement had the same social origins as the intelligentsia. Many of the early revolutionaries – young men and a surprising number of women – came from noble families. But their number soon grew with the advent of the *raznochintsy* (men of different ranks) who flooded the universities. They came from merchant or even peasant families; many were of mixed stock – illegitimate children of noblemen or of rich landowners and peasant women.

These early revolutionaries of the mid-nineteenth century had borrowed their ideas from French utopian writers such as Fourier and Saint-Simon. To these ideas they added the peculiarly Russian preoccupation with the liberation of the serfs. They called themselves *Narodniki* (Populists) and in fact their first mass action was the 'going to the people'. Groups of young men and women invaded the countryside, intent on bringing notions of freedom to the peasants. It was a fiasco, as the peasants did not trust them. The secret police had no difficulty in tracking them down, and the prisons were soon filled with these young idealists.

Soon there was more rewarding work to be done. By now large cities had factories and a growing urban proletariat. Many revolutionaries directed their energies to converting groups of workers to their ideas. It was dangerous work. The factories were situated outside the city gates. Most workers were housed in barracks, and both the gates and the barracks were closely watched by agents of the secret police. Prince Kropotkin, the future leader of the Anarchists, was one of those early propagandists. He was a page at the imperial court, and he has described how, when he went 'beyond the gates' straight from his duties, he would exchange his court costume for a worker's garb, complete with cap and bag of tools. Kropotkin too landed in gaol.

Before long new forces began to make themselves felt. When, in the early 1860s, Tsar Alexander II introduced substantial reforms, including the emancipation of the serfs, the public response was enthusiastic. But there were also complaints that the reforms did not go far enough – and that so alarmed the Tsar and his advisers that they tried to go back on what they had done. That in turn evoked widespread disappointment and anger, and in the end the Tsar was assassinated. Executions and imprisonments followed, and on the surface public order seemed to be restored. Nevertheless, discontent grew and grew. Groups of students and young professional men and women met in secret to discuss past mistakes and future possibilities for radical change.

One of the main complaints was that reform had pauperised the peasants: it had emancipated the peasants from serfdom but had failed to provide them with the land they needed to survive. As a result, masses of the poorest peasants invaded the towns in search of work. In a time of rapid industrialisation work was easy to find, in one or other of the new factories. However, these people were not only poor, they were illiterate. The fight against illiteracy now became a central preoccupation of both the liberal and the radical intelligentsia.

While the liberal country gentry founded schools in the villages, in the towns groups of students taught reading and writing to the urban poor. When in the late 1890s several Marxist groups were formed in St Petersburg – including one to which both Lenin and Yuly Martov belonged – they too found that the first step towards the emancipation of the proletariat had to be the spread of literacy. Nadezhda Krupskaya, who was to become Lenin's wife, belonged to a group of young women who taught workers to read and write. And this was typical. It was by the same route that both my parents entered on their revolutionary careers.

Both my parents were Jews. Though they were agnostics and took no part in Jewish religious life, they both felt very Jewish. Both spoke fluent Yiddish and loved the pithiness which is so characteristic of Yiddish speech and writing. For them being Jewish was the most natural thing in the world and something to be proud of. Nevertheless, to be Jewish in tsarist Russia meant that one belonged to a disadvantaged ethnic minority. There were many such minorities – the Ukrainians, Georgians and Balts were all discriminated against – but the Jews suffered under even greater disadvant-ages than the others.

Jews were residentially restricted to the so-called Pale of Jewish Settlement on the western fringe of the empire, and were not allowed to reside elsewhere unless they were accepted at a university or had professional qualifications that made them useful to Russian society. Doctors, pharma-cists and even professional gardeners were allowed to settle in Russian cities, including the two capitals. But to acquire such qualifications, unless one went abroad, was in itself very difficult. In order to enter a Russian university, Jewish boys had to finish a Russian school with a gold medal – and this despite the overt anti-Semitism of the school authorities. No wonder that only the brightest and most determined Jewish boys made it.

Jewish women harbouring similar ambitions had even greater obstacles to overcome. Russian women in general were debarred from higher education. It is true that in liberal circles there was widespread sympathy with women's desire for such education: several professors, including the celebrated composer Borodin (who was also a professor of medicine), were happy to invite women to their lectures. The fact remained that only two degree courses were open to them: midwifery and pharmacology.

My parents came from Svenciany, near Vilna (now Vilnius, Lithuania), in the Pale of Jewish Settlement. This was the area along the western borders of the Russian empire to which Jews were confined, and where they lived in uneasy coexistence with other minorities – Lithuanians, Poles and Ukrainians. Svenciany was a *shtetl*, as small towns in the Pale were called in Yiddish. Life there was encompassed by the synagogue and by small trading. To escape from this stifling place into the wider world of knowledge and ideas and to join the student fraternity, where members of all minorities, including Jews, were accepted as equals in a spirit of comradeship – that was the dream of both my parents.

Father was the first to fulfil it. It was made easier for him when his family moved to the large town of Vilna. His father, a cultured and liberal man who became a respected attorney in Vilna, was able to send his sons to the best Russian school in town. And in due course my father received his gold medal and went to St Petersburg, where he was lucky to find a vacancy at the Technological Institute. What a triumph this was! How eagerly he breathed the air of that great city, visited the places connected with the names of great Russian writers and thinkers! A handsome, broad-shouldered young man, fair haired, with merry blue eyes – Lithuanian Jews were often blond – he was popular with Russian students.

Universities were then hotbeds of radicalism, and soon he too was engulfed in the revolutionary movement. The date was the late 1890s and there were already various Marxist groups in existence. These groups were concerned above all with the industrial working class, whereas other, non-Marxist socialist groups still focused on the peasantry. Revolutionary activity among the workers consisted in the first instance in instructing small groups of factory workers, often simply in reading and writing, sometimes also in elementary history. My father entered enthusiastically into this work; together with a few friends he set out to assemble books for a circulating library for workers. This was of course a subversive activity. The police soon discovered what was going on, the books were confiscated, some of the organisers were arrested and others went into hiding.

If it was difficult for a Jewish boy to reach St Petersburg, it was doubly so for a Jewish girl such as my mother. Eva Gordón (a common Russian–Jewish surname, quite unconnected with the Scottish Gordon) had early in life decided to escape from the narrow world of the *shtetl*. Since the only way to do that was to get a degree, she chose pharmacology and at barely fifteen years of age apprenticed herself to a pharmacist in Dvinsk. Dvinsk was a district town in the Pale with a very orthodox Jewish community – my mother was stoned when she dared to carry an umbrella on Saturday. Her pay was poor and the working hours nine in the morning to nine in the evening and even later. At night she studied for her degree and read widely. She found a few kindred spirits among the local students and sometimes joined them for a convivial evening or a picnic in the country. After three years in Dvinsk she went to Kazan where she was to take her finals as an external student. She had to borrow the price of the ticket to Kazan and there, after paying her fees, she lived at almost starvation level. Still, at the end of the year she passed her examinations. She went at once to St Petersburg.

She knew nobody there except Mark Broido, her child-hood friend, and it was a great blow to find that he had vanished. However, she was not daunted and before long she had found a modest room and a job at a pharmacy. She settled down to wait and soon things began to happen. One day a few young workers came to her and explained that they had got used to their 'Little Workers' Library' and were missing it very much. They knew that the chaps who had organised it were either in prison or in hiding, but could she get them some books and build up a new collection? She had no experience of such work but she was eager to help. Soon Mark Broido surfaced and more helpers appeared. In no time at all my mother found herself an active member of the revolutionary underground. It was an exciting and dangerous life, to be always on the move, changing addresses and disguises and often one's very name; playing hide-and-seek with the police, dodging arrest and not always succeeding. But it offered more than excitement: my mother had the satisfaction of being treated by men as an equal. For in the revolutionary move-ment, and only there, women were accepted as equals.

The inevitable catastrophe struck in January 1901, when the whole group was rounded up, put in prison and sent into exile in the remotest north-eastern corner of Siberia.

The usual procedure of going into Siberian exile was known as 'travelling by stages' in large groups under military guards.

Stages were shorter or longer stops on the way – some for just one night – at small prison compounds or at large transit prisons. Throughout the nineteenth century the exiles walked the whole way, often in chains, but later it became more usual to go by prison trains. And later still it even became possible for political exiles to pay their own fares and to travel by ordinary passenger trains, without a gendarme in the compartment. But the transit prisons were still there and it was at one of these large prisons, where prisoners, political and criminal, were regrouped for diverse destinations, that my mother and father met again after their arrest, and it was there, in the prison office, that they were married. For the bride it was a second marriage – at some time in her young life she had married and borne two daughters, Alexandra (Sanya) and Galina (Galya); but the marriage was dissolved after the husband became mentally deranged. He never reappeared in my mother's life and the two girls found in my father a most tender and loving parent. Now she was marrying her childhood sweetheart, the boy from next door.

It was an unusual wedding. The prison governor had arranged for a religious ceremony in his office and though both bride and groom were agnostics, they chose the Jewish rites. These, however, necessitated the presence of ten Jews, and they were difficult to find. However, a mixed lot of Jewish criminals and politicals were finally rounded up and the ceremony could begin. But now it turned out that the bridegroom had no ring. The bride had to borrow one from an old vagrant woman who was sitting in the prison office: it was a small ring made of plain iron. After the ceremony the bride and bridegroom returned to their respective cells.

In the memoirs that my mother wrote many years later, in foreign exile, she describes the wedding, the subsequent journey and the arrival in a small town in the frozen north, where her mother soon joined them, bringing the two little girls with her. There, at the coldest spot of the northern hemisphere, my brother Daniel (Danya) was born. But it was not their final destination: they had to complete a most trying and perilous journey in river barges before they reached the town of Yakutsk. In all, the journey had lasted more than a year.

The town of Yakutsk was the administrative centre of the vast Yakutsk region. My family album shows on its first page two photos of my family in front of its Yakutsk loghouse home. In one my father is seated and is holding his two step-daughters on his knees; both have shaved heads because of the danger of lice. In the other photo, my grandmother, seated on the top step before the front door of the house, is holding my baby brother, while my mother, sitting below her, is half-turned towards the camera. Not a beauty, my mother, but her face is striking and there is an unselfconscious grace in the posture of her body. The photos must have been taken during the short Arctic summer, because for six winter months there was complete darkness in Yakutsk and semi-darkness for the short spring and autumn. Before the onset of winter enough logs, water and milk and all other necessities had to be purchased and stored in the roomy porch of the house. For in winter nobody could walk out of doors for longer than a few minutes, because breath froze in the mouth and the nostrils.

Yakutsk was overcrowded with political exiles and more and more were arriving all the time. The authorities thought they had solved the housing problem by dispersing male exiles, including my father, to small hamlets in the region. The native Yakuts who lived in these hamlets did not welcome newcomers; they lived in yurts (large tents covered in horse hide) which they shared with their cattle, and there was little space and no food to spare. The exiles responded in their own fashion: each morning soldiers escorted them out of town and every evening, unescorted, they returned. But resentment among the exiles grew and grew, until it exploded in mutiny. The exiles barricaded themselves in a loghouse; it belonged to a merchant called Romanov, so the mutiny became known as the Romanovka. The authorities ordered the soldiers to shoot, with the result that one of the mutineers was killed. Only when the loghouse was riddled with holes like a sieve did the mutineers surrender. They were marched to prison, where they remained until their trial.

My family album shows a happy group of smiling men and women prisoners and two little girls sitting on the ground in front. These were my two half-sisters, whom my mother brought to the prison every morning on her way to work. She had not been able to join the others in their besieged house because she was breastfeeding the baby, so she was instead assigned liaison and supply duties outside. The two girls had the time of their lives in prison: the events in far-away Yakutsk had received international acclaim and socialists from France and Italy were sending boxes of oranges and other fruit to the Yakutsk prison. Most of the choicest titbits were fed to the two children. Years later – so the story goes – my sister Galya, when asked where she would most like to be, answered without hesitation: 'In prison'.

At their trial, the mutineers were sentenced to eight years' hard labour but my father, accused of shooting and wounding a soldier, faced a retrial and a possible death sentence. To begin with, however, they were all, families included, loaded on to horse carts and a long, slow caravan of these carts set out on a long journey to the central prison of Alexandrovsk, near Irkutsk, the capital of eastern Siberia. My mother describes how at every stop – for lunch break or for the night – the 'passengers' deliberately changed places, so as to annoy and confuse the convoy guards who were supposed to count them on each occasion and could somehow never get the sum right. My father was one of several men who 'went missing' on the journey. For four days and nights he walked through the dense Siberian taiga, dodging, in the words of the famous Siberian convict song, 'wild beasts and the soldiers' bullets'. Finally, completely exhausted and half-starved, he chanced upon a small railway stop, with just one small shed for a station. Finding the shed empty my father walked in, stretched himself out on a wooden bench and went to sleep. He was woken up – after how long a time? – by the noise of an approaching engine and by a railway official shaking him roughly and urging him to hurry, if he wanted to catch his train. So, willy-nilly, he boarded the train and travelled in comfort to the next stop, a biggish station. He could see police on the platform, looking the passengers over, so he melted away unnoticed. By this time he was near civilisation and able to contact comrades, get clean clothes, some money and a different identity. He managed the weeks of travel right across Siberia and Russia without being detected. Finally he was smuggled across the border.

Meanwhile my mother had been brought to the central prison where, as soon as she learned that my father was out of danger, she promptly organised her own escape and for Grandmother Sara to take the children. Helped by comrades inside and outside the prison, she set out to reach the railway at Irkutsk. She had always prided herself on her talent for disguise and impersonation, and this now stood her in good stead. First she assumed the part of a poor woman who had been deserted by her husband, then that of a rich merchant's wife, dressed in furs and travelling in a fast troika. Once on the train she became a rather frivolous, flirtatious young lady. At every point she was in danger of recapture, but such was her ingenuity that she succeeded in traversing the whole of the immense Russian empire – Siberia, Russia and Poland – without ever being detected. In Warsaw she was again helped by comrades to reach the border, where she was literally carried, on the back of a smuggler, across a river and into German territory.

My parents had planned to meet up in Vienna, but in the event the meeting took place in London. After a short stay there they returned to Russia to resume their revolutionary work. On the way they stopped in Switzerland, the centre of Russian socialist emigration. Here they found the leaders of the Marxist movement, Georgy Plekhanov, Pavel Axelrod, Vera Zasulich, Martov and Lenin, who together were publishing the famous journal *Iskra* (The Spark). They also learned that during their years in the Siberian wilderness the Russian Social Democratic Workers' Party had been founded. At the founding congress the entire leadership had been arrested, but in 1903 a second congress was convened, this time in London. Now the two youngest members of the executive, Martov and

Lenin, fell out over an issue which at the time seemed of little importance but which later turned out to be all-important. It concerned the nature of the party. Martov insisted on a democratic structure, Lenin on an autocratic one. Over this issue the party split into Lenin's Bolsheviks and Martov's Mensheviks. After listening to all the arguments, my parents opted for the Mensheviks. But what they wanted above all to know was where in Russia they could be most usefully employed. On learning of the situation in the oilfields of Baku, in the Caucasus, they decided to go there.

In Baku the workforce included Russians, Georgians, Persians, Armenians and Tartars. The Tartars, who were the original inhabitants of the land, held a privileged position: they were employed as armed watchmen in the oilfields and exercised a reign of terror over everyone else, especially all workers' organisations. Nevertheless, the Social Democrats were able to build up a Union of Baku Workers, with thousands of members and its own clandestine printing press; my parents played an important part in this work. It was a dangerous life: my mother could never go out except escorted by two or three men, and with a revolver stuck in her belt. Even then she was in constant danger of being murdered by the Tartars. In the end a terrible massacre of Armenians by the Tartars, accompanied by huge material destruction on the oilfields, forced my parents to leave Baku.

After a short stay in Moscow my parents returned to St Petersburg. There they found enormous changes in the political atmosphere. The year, 1905, had started peaceably enough. On 22 January, an Orthodox priest, Father Gapon, was carrying a petition which, in accordance with a time-honoured Russian custom, was meant to be presented directly to the Tsar. The crowd following him was larger than usual and the authorities panicked. When Father Gapon reached the wide space in front of the Winter Palace, the troops were ordered to open fire. Within seconds the ground was littered with bodies. The shock of this event roused the country to a new political awareness. Throughout the year mass meetings and demonstrations took place all over Russia. In Moscow detachments of the army mutinied and so did the sailors of the battleship *Potemkin* in Odessa, an episode immortalised by Eisenstein's famous film.

The very texture of social and political life changed. There were several new political parties, legal and illegal. The largest was the KD (Constitutional Democrats), which campaigned for the establishment of parliamentary democracy under a constitutional monarchy. There were widespread demands for freedom of the press and of assembly. Innumerable societies sprang up, of students, of women, of professional men. At political meetings workers joined trade unions and went on strike. Faced with all this turmoil, the government created a union of its own, the Union of the Russian People, the notorious Black Hundreds. Its ranks were made up of thugs, police, spies and provocateurs and its principal activity was organising and carrying out pogroms.

Throughout the year tension mounted. The socialist parties, which were of course all illegal, tried to organise concerted action. They formed elected bodies, such as co-operative societies, trade unions and soviets. The last, which were a Menshevik innovation, were intended to become a sort of parliament to which factory workers would send their deputies. In the event the entire St Petersburg soviet was arrested. All over the country demonstrations met with brutal suppression. There were mass arrests and executions. In Moscow some 2500 workers perished on the barricades.

In the end the government was forced to make concessions. However, they were very half-hearted concessions. A Duma, or parliament, was established but it was granted only a consultative role, and elected deputies enjoyed no immunity from arrest. Nor was the whole arrangement at all stable. Whenever the Tsar was displeased with the conduct of the Duma he simply dissolved it and convened a new Duma. In all there were four successive Dumas.

These were years of great expectations and great disappointments for Russian society as a whole. They were also years of great vitality. The arts were flourishing: there were new composers, playwrights, theatres, painters. The Constitutional Democrats and other liberal parties were learning their first lessons in parliamentary democracy. The illegal socialist parties were competing for leadership of the emerging industrial working class. The oldest, the Social Revolutionary Party, which traditionally had been oriented towards the peasantry, was now gaining a foothold in the factories. The Social Democratic Workers' Party, though still headed by a joint central committee, was in fact more and more divided, with the Mensheviks and Bolsheviks at war with one another.

Both my parents were immersed in party work. There was still elementary teaching to be done but there were also more advanced courses, particularly in the history of the Western working-class movement. It was gratifying to see how many talented workers came to the fore. Both my parents also had their special interests. My father was very active in the creation of mutual aid societies, trade unions and soviets. He was elected to the executive of the St Petersburg soviet and, like the rest of that body, was arrested and briefly imprisoned in December 1905. My mother's special interest was in the economic and social situation of working women, about which she later wrote a book.

Above all, there was continual electioneering – for the Duma, the soviets, the trade unions, the factory committees – and all the socialist parties took part. My mother told me of one memorable incident. At a mass meeting at the Baltic shipbuilding wharf, the Mensheviks and Bolsheviks expressed opposite views: the Mensheviks were for, the Bolsheviks against participation in elections to the Duma. It had been agreed that my mother should speak on behalf of the Mensheviks, Grigory Zinoviev on behalf of the Bolsheviks. But without previous notification Zinoviev brought Lenin with him, to speak against participation. My mother regarded herself as a mediocre orator and certainly no match for the formidable Lenin – and when she began to speak, her voice seemed to fail her. Nevertheless, in the event she carried the meeting with her, defeating Lenin by fifty votes to thirteen.

2

I WAS BORN on 7 October 1907 (Old Style calendar), as my mother's fourth and last child. Mother told me that I was born on the stroke of midnight; ever since I have claimed two birthdays. She also told me that at the time of my birth Father was hiding from the police in Finland. There was, of course, no way of reaching him – but just then a Menshevik from Moscow, Vasily Sher, appeared unannounced on the doorstep, on the run from the Moscow police. Mother immediately dispatched him to Finland, to find my father and tell him the glad news. No sooner had he departed than an unknown comrade arrived from Moscow just too late to inform him that his own wife too had just given birth to a daughter.

Mother was a good and loving mother when she was there, also a splendid cook and hostess – again when she was there.

Most of the time she simply was not there, nor was Father. Even when they were at home, they were both frantically busy trying to earn. They worked at translating, from English and German into Russian. That was their sole source of income and though it was comparatively well paid, it did not bring in enough. Often our grandmother had to help out by cooking meals, inexpensive and healthy, for students.

Our maternal grandmother, Sara, was a far more constant presence than Mother or Father. Only occasionally did she return to her own home and husband in Lithuania; most of the time she was completely involved in her daughter's life and us. To us children she was an ever-present source of tender care. She was dearly loved by all of us and also by our parents' many comrades. Years later Father's youngest sister, who often stayed with us, said to me, 'Babushka Sara was a saint'. It was Sara who held our family together. It was she who, when Mother escaped from Siberia and fled to England, journeyed with the two little girls and the baby all the way from Irkutsk to Lithuania. And it was she who looked after the family when my mother was exiled to Siberia again, a few years before the Revolution.

At the time of my birth we were living in Lesnoye, a suburb of St Petersburg, where my parents had rented a large house with a large garden. I remember little from that early period of my life. But there was a Christmas, when I was aged just three, which we Jewish children were invited to celebrate with a working-class family who also lived in Lesnoye. The husband was a comrade of my parents and the couple made us very welcome. The Christmas tree with its bright decorations and flickering candles was like something out of a fairytale. I was spellbound as I sat beneath it with my sisters and brother, who cracked nuts for me and fed me on sweet biscuits.

To go into the city we had to take a steam-tram. I have two memories connected with that journey. In one, I am travelling on the tram and the conductor puts me next to him on the front platform, where passengers are not allowed, and tells me to take the steering wheel. I am quite breathless with pride – and with anxiety. My other memory is traumatic. I am taken to St Petersburg, to a big house and a strange room; it looks to me like a large cage divided by high wire partitions. We stand in the middle, while in the passageway on the other side of the partitions stand several men, some quite near the wire, others further back. One of the men near the wire has a long beard. I don't know that man. When Mother lifts me in her arms towards him and I hear him calling me his Verochka, his little darling, I shrink back in horror and scream. I turn my head away; I won't look at him and Mother has to take me away. Later I was told that all this happened while Father was serving two years' imprisonment, spent in solitary confinement, as punishment for his escape from Siberia.

When I was four or five years old the family moved to St Petersburg, to an apartment close to the River Neva. We had no nurses or governesses but no matter: we children learned to read and write by four and had read most of the world's classics in translation by twelve. And my sisters and brother went to very good schools. In Lesnoye they went to a progressive co-educational school with facilities for sport and all kinds of athletics: my sister Sanya became an excellent athlete. Our summer holidays were spent cheaply but healthily either near the beautiful Finnish lakes or in the magnificent Lithuanian forests.

When my parents were both at home in St Petersburg life centred on the dining-room. In the afternoon and late into the evening Mother would preside over the large table with the inexhaustible samovar next to her. There were always several invited guests and more would drop in uninvited; it is a Russian custom to drop in on friends 'when there is a light in the window'.

My parents were of very different temperaments. Whereas Mother was all action, Father had a contemplative side. I remember Mother's favourite lullaby, which she sang to me at bedtime. It was in Russian and went like this:

> The mother of the four winds greeted the youngest
>   when he came home:
> 'Where have you been, my son, what have you been
>   doing?'
> 'I have been blasting the rocks in the mountains,
> I have been whipping up waves in the sea.'
> 'But now you have to calm down and rock this
>   cradle for me.'

When Father put me to bed he sang a sad, gentle lullaby in Yiddish:

> Dreams may tell you that you will build bridges
>   and encircle the world,
> But life will teach you that you will be trading in
>   raisins and almonds.

Though Father had a well-deserved reputation for energy and courage, his nature was essentially that of a scholar.

During his time in solitary confinement he was allowed only one book, the Bible. He turned this restriction to advantage by ordering several bilingual editions. In this way he taught himself French and Italian and improved his German and English. He also loved poetry and knew many poems, Russian and foreign, by heart. I well remember Mother complaining that when she was busy rolling pastry in the kitchen, he would follow her around, reciting from Dante: '*Nel mezzo del cammin di nostra vita*', and so on.

There was, in our St Petersburg home, a spacious playroom. But while the other three children each had a special corner allotted them, where they kept their books and games and which they guarded jealously from one another, there did not seem to be any particular place for me: the door was in the fourth corner. Even when the others were away at school I rarely played there, feeling like an intruder. I much preferred playing in the long, dark corridor that connected the playroom to the entrance hall or better still in the hall itself. The fact that many doors led from it and into it and could be opened and shut, offered so many possibilities. And when all the doors were shut, it was dark and secret like a cave.

I had my own games. I loved, as most girls do, to play mother and baby, only I never played with dolls, particularly not with the over-bright, over-dressed doll sent by my uncle and aunt from Vienna. My babies were cushions carefully rolled and bandaged into a kind of sausage, and the heavier and more unwieldy they were, the more tenderly I loved them. I also loved building houses or even whole streets with pots and pans borrowed from the kitchen. Better still I planned whole neighbourhoods in my mind and could sometimes be observed, Mother told me, turning imaginary corners, crossing imaginary bridges and so on, while keeping up an interminable murmured commentary.

I don't remember feeling lonely, even when the whole family was out. I was quite content to play in the hall, from where I could hear the voice of our maid Nastya in the kitchen. I loved listening to the symphony of kitchen sounds; pots and pans being washed up or filled with water or shuffled on the stove, the muffled movements of the rolling-pin on the pastry board. And then those songs, the unforgettable songs of Russian kitchenmaids, all about broken vows and broken hearts, and poison and death:

> The evening light was fading,
> The street lamps were being lit;
> My love, he is not coming . . .
> But my poison is at hand . . .
> Marusya drank the poison,
> the ambulance took her away;
> her lover, he found her dying
> And this is what he said . . .

or

> 'My poison cost me but little
> a small box of matches will do;
> and my young life is utterly worthless,
> I ruined it a long time ago.'

I was moved to tears listening outside the kitchen door.

Another entertainment of a high calibre was provided by the arrival of the floor polishers. All apartment houses in St Petersburg had parquet flooring, as had some of the main streets, and floor polishing was a high art. It was usually three young men who came. They strapped a thick polishing cloth impregnated with wax to one foot and then performed, arms crossed at the back, an intricately rhythmic and to my mind very beautiful dance, gliding forwards and backwards with supple grace. When many years later I saw Fred Astaire, I was reminded of that very different kind of elegant ballet.

When my sisters and brother were at home, Danya usually recruited me for his boisterous game of soldiers and battles or trains and collisions. He assigned the least heroic parts to me, and in the end usually chased me away altogether, complaining that I was useless and a cry-baby. All the while my sister Sanya, the eldest, was stretched out full-length on a couch in her corner, devouring one of the novels by Jules Verne, her all-time favourite author, and took little notice of anything. When we got too noisy she groped blindly for some kind of missile, book, shoe or anything handy and flung it at us without taking her eyes off the page. In the other corner Galya only smiled. I liked her gentle quiet ways much better but she was secretive, a person apart. She was a mathematical prodigy. At sixteen she left school to become assistant to the professor of mathematics at St Petersburg University; at seventeen or eighteen she died of meningitis, while my mother was once again in exile in Siberia.

The only time that all four of us children were involved was when Vasily Kondratievich came on one of his visits. I don't know when he first came into our lives, but by the time I was six or seven, there was a well-established routine. He would arrive on any day and at any time, without previous warning, carrying only a shabby little rucksack, and stand humbly by the front door while Mother would try to discourage him: 'The guest room isn't free', or 'There's no camp bed even', to which he would reply that he would only stay a few nights and that he could easily sleep on the floor. We all knew that Mother did not have the heart to refuse and he would stay, not a few nights but for two or three weeks.

I was so often told the story of Vasily Kondratievich's life that it was engraved on my memory forever. He was an illiterate peasant boy, an orphan, when he met on the road a group of geographers with their fascinating equipment and attached himself to them. By the time they had become aware of the little ragged, barefoot fellow, they had gone a long way from his village. And when he assured them that he would not be missed, having no family to miss him, they took him along with them. So began his career as a member of scientific expeditions, first as a general dogsbody but by slow degrees as a store-master and eventually as a scientist. He turned out to be a quick learner. He even drew a regular salary. He was happy wandering around the country with his companions, spending nights around the campfire and listening to their talk. The trouble came when work was at an end, the expedition returned to St Petersburg to hand in the results and the members dispersed to their homes and families. It was then that the orphan boy felt very forsaken and alone. I don't know how he found us; there must have been a first time when Mother perhaps invited him and he made friends with us children and stayed on. Shy with grown-ups, he was completely at ease with us, even witty and talkative. We considered him, rightly, as our friend.

Once the argument was won and Mother had relented, we erupted like a volcano from whatever room we had been listening from and stormed him like a fortress. We conducted him in triumph to the guest room and overwhelmed him with questions: where had he been, how long could he stay and what had he brought us? The answers to all our queries were never given at once. 'First things first,' he would say and, opening his little rucksack, would carefully extract what seemed to us a huge wad of money and keeping only a small amount for himself would carry the bulk to Mother for safe-keeping. Then he told us to be good and disappeared for hours, reappearing later with several heavy sacks full of samples of stone and soil. (It was this that made him such a problematic guest in Mother's eyes.) We were dancing with impatience to see the contents, knowing also that this was not all. And indeed, soon the doorbell rang and there was a boy delivering a whole tray of cakes from the Filipov patisserie, the best in town. Vasily Kondratievich never bought less than a whole tray, sometimes several, and we had to promise Mother not to over-eat and make ourselves sick. Another boy delivered a sack of nuts.

When the samples were all unpacked (there was a remarkable scarcity of personal belongings), the table would be pushed into the middle of the guest room, chairs would be placed round it and we would solemnly proceed to gamble – for nuts. Sanya was a daring gambler, Danya a cautious one, Galya a calculating one. I, who did not know how to play even the simplest nursery games, usually sat on Vasily Kondratievich's knee while he 'advised' me how to play my hand. I was supposed to be his 'fiancée', and he made up endless doggerel rhymes for me, all about how Vaska fell in love with Verochka and how he won her. They usually started with: 'There once lived a little girl, Vera . . .'. The most perfect of his poems was however not about me but about a fictitious little girl, Kappa:

> There was once a little girl, Kappa,
> she owned a rhinoceros and a hat.
> The rhinoceros was of porcelain
> while the hat was of the latest fashion –
> and both resided on the mantelpiece.
> The hat covered the rhinoceros
> and the rhinoceros prayed to God:
> 'Lord, deliver me from this hat –
> I don't want a hat of high fashion
> but I do want a life of freedom.'

I loved his verses. In Russian they rhymed and had an attractive beat.

As Vasily Kondratievich stayed on and on, the floor of the guest room got dirtier and dirtier from his samples, while we, the children, developed tummy upsets from eating too many creamy cakes. Still, when his expedition was once again ready to set out and he left us, we all lamented his departure, even our maid Nastya, who assured Mother that she would soon get the guest room sparkling clean again.

I remember our family holidays in Lithuania. On the way we usually spent a few days with our paternal grandparents in the ancient capital of Lithuania, Vilna. I was a bit shy of the large apartment with its dark furniture and could never warm to the caresses of my grandmother, whom I barely knew; she was a little dark lady, stiff in black, with a black wig such as devout Jewesses always wore. But I was at ease with my grandfather, whom I thought beautiful, the most beautiful man I knew, with his white beard, long and full and soft. He had laughing eyes and smiled at me so tenderly.

From Vilna we went on to the home of our maternal grandparents in the *shtetl* of Svenciany. For me the main attraction there was the timber yard belonging to our grandparents. Facing the street there stood their house with its many windows and next to it a wide, heavy gate through which carts and wagons drove past a sort of garden, to the timber yard proper. At the entrance to the yard there was a small house known as the office, in which our grandfather sat all day long. He sat on a high stool before a kind of lectern on which lay the Talmud, open on a page dark with age. I never saw him turning this page and indeed Mother told me that it was the same page that he was reading when she was a child, only it was even darker now. He never seemed to leave the high stool and after the first greeting in the morning, when he gave us an abstracted gentle smile, he never talked to us. In later years I wondered whether he had always been the same or was it that he had been so devastated by the death of his first wife and their three sons that he did not care for life thereafter? This did not quite fit as he had married again, our grandmother Sara, and had a son, Naum, and a daughter, Eva, by her. But obviously at some stage he turned away from life and took to the Talmud, not reading it but nodding over it, rhythmically, in the manner of rabbinical scholars. He left the running of the timber yard entirely to his wife.

The timber yard was an ideal place to be in, a paradise, a vast expanse filled with uncut logs and freshly cut planks, all piled up neatly to make narrow passages between their ranks. Nothing delighted me more than the smell of the freshly cut timber. I would climb up to the top of a pile of planks and sit there smelling it. The ranks of logs and timber made wonderful passages and places to hide and to play all kinds of games. Simply climbing up and sitting on top was a lovely pastime, and it offered the bonus that one could look over the wooden fence and into the next-door yard. That was a place which hired out horse carriages, so there were always horses going out and returning, being watered and brushed down and led into the stables. There were also small light carriages and commodious family barouches standing about. And there was always plenty of movement and noise.

The summer was spent in a forester's house on a lake in the heart of the virgin forest. There was not another house for miles around and our only visitor was the forester himself, who lived in another part of the forest. The main attraction for the rest of my family was the boat on the lake but I was afraid of water and much preferred to go on gentle rambles through the woods, walking under high trees in semi-darkness and then coming to a warm, sunlit clearing, full of wild strawberries, raspberries or mushrooms, according to season. This was the best place to stop and sit or lie down and get warm in the sun, while the strong smell of grasses, flowers and berries made one drowsy. Time stood still. The day of departure came much too soon and it was always with a pang that we returned to St Petersburg.

3

I REALISE NOW that when I was small, places were more vivid to me than people. But for the photos in our family album, could I put faces to any of the people in my early childhood? They were mere shadows. Those closest to me were perhaps more distinct; they were definite presences. And though often they turned into absences like Mother and Father, Vasily Kondratievich and even Nastya (who might leave and be replaced by Marusya), they had a semi-permanence, a solidity of a kind and I was aware of them. But most other people hardly existed for me. Only much later, at the age of seven or eight, did I notice strangers, stepping, as it were, out of the shadows or wings into full light.

Places, on the other hand, always had an immediate and enduring impact. The inside and outside of houses, streets, squares, crossroads, evoked a lively response and feelings akin to affection, even love. Throughout my life I have had love affairs with cities and towns. First St Petersburg, then Kuragino and Minusinsk in Siberia and then many foreign cities.

Our apartment in St Petersburg was on the Bolshoy Prospekt, a district situated on the unfashionable side of the River Neva. However if *they* had the Senate Square and the Nevsky Prospekt and the Admiralty arch and spire, St Isaac's Cathedral and the splendid Winter Palace, *we* had the Peter and Paul Fortress and the Uspensky Cathedral and, on the neighbouring Vasilievsky Island, the University. In any case, the views of the city were equally beautiful from both shores. Apart from a few palaces and ceremonial buildings and squares, St Petersburg was a city of apartment houses, four or five storeys high, lining wide streets and built around one or several interlinking courtyards. There were no trees in these courtyards and little light. But children could play in the little gardens laid out around churches, and our nearest playground was the garden of the Uspensky Cathedral. Hither I walked every morning, hand in hand with Nastya. My other hand clutched tightly a coin with which to buy my mid-morning snack. Ten kopeks bought me a pastry or *pirozhok* (meat pie) from Filipov's patisserie, while on other days five kopeks could be spent on the equally delicious buttered slice of freshly baked bread.

The Bolshoy Prospekt was the main thoroughfare of our district, and the famous patisserie was only a little way from our house. To enter it was for me like entering wonderland; it was all gold and tall engraved mirrors and glistening chandeliers. But most awe-inspiring of all were the displays of cakes and pastries. Behind the wide mahogany counters there were equally wide sloping shelves on which huge trays with pastries, cream cakes or *pirozhki* (little pies) were displayed. As soon as a tray was half-empty, white-coated kitchen boys appeared from nowhere to replace them with full ones. It was torture to have to choose. There were so many varieties, just of the *pirozhki*, made with yeast, puff or other pastry, mincemeat or rice or cabbage or lights or fish, all delicately seasoned with onions and hard-boiled eggs and parsley. Of the little cakes there was such an infinite choice that I usually just plunged for any on the first tray.

On alternate days Nastya and I went to a small basement grocery around the corner. The side streets of St Petersburg had many such small shops: cobblers', laundry, grocery or liquor stores, to which one had to descend some six or ten steep but wide steps from the sidewalk. These little shops were frequented mainly by artisans, apprentices, servants and the like. We went there to buy our two huge slices of buttered, freshly baked white bread. It was delivered around midday by a chubby youth pushing a two-wheeled cart with several enormous steaming hot loaves on a large wooden tray. There were always quite a few people waiting for it and more crowded into the small over-stocked shop to inhale the delicious hot smell of freshly baked bread and to watch the shopkeeper, in a stiff apron of white linen, carve the bread into slices, slap on yellow butter from a chunk on the counter and hand a piece to each of us in a square of crinkly paper. It was heaven.

These daily walks to the little gardens around the Uspensky Cathedral were the beginning of my exploration of St

Petersburg and many years were to pass before it could be resumed. I was not yet seven years of age when the First World War broke out. It found Russian socialists divided: while some argued that it was right to defend one's country against unprovoked aggression, others were totally opposed to participation in any war. The former group called themselves Defensists, the latter Internationalists. My parents disagreed on this vitally important matter, Father being a Defensist, Mother an Internationalist.

Many Internationalists were arrested, Mother among them. She was so often away from home for long periods that I hardly noticed her absence and no-one explained what had happened to her. So it came as somewhat of a shock when one morning Mother reappeared unannounced. The flat was empty but for me and Nastya. Nastya could be heard shouting through the kitchen window to another maid across the yard and I was playing, as so often, in the large, dark entrance hall. As far as I remember I was 'moving house' that morning and had dragged a few empty suitcases and cartons from their usual place in the guest room, when the front bell rang. It was Nastya's job to answer the door but she could be heard still conversing loudly with her friend; she had heard nothing. So I opened the door and there was Mother with a suitcase and a bundle in her hands, looking pale and thin in the semi-darkness of the landing, like a ghost. 'Verochka!' She quickly came in, closed the door behind her and drew me to her. We both sat down on her case and cried. I always cried when she reappeared though I don't think that I cried or missed her very much in between. Each time she seemed a stranger at first and I felt a bit shy of her but a good cry seemed to bring us together again.

Soon the flat was full of people, Father, the children and innumerable friends and comrades. It appeared that she had been released from prison for just one week, to prepare for her journey. She had been 'administratively' (without trial) sentenced to three years' exile in western Siberia, the exact locality to be assigned courtesy of the governor of western Siberia. A week was not a very long time to settle all the family affairs. It was decided between my parents that the elder children should remain in St Petersburg, under the care of Father and Grandmother Sara and continue their schooling, while I was to go with Mother. My brother Danya was to go with us for the summer, as the long vacation was not far away, and return to school in the autumn.

Since Mother's first journey to Siberia the treatment of political prisoners had become much more humane; now she was able to get permission to travel in an ordinary train instead of a prison train. Naturally she had to pay for her own and our tickets, which must have strained the family finances considerably.

Of this and other practical problems I knew nothing. My only worry was which toys to take with me, since we could carry only a limited amount of luggage. Danya was similarly preoccupied. The week passed quickly and we were on the train to Moscow and from there on a train on the Trans-Siberian Railway. I imagine we were travelling third class but we found it palatial. We had a whole compartment to ourselves. Most of the time my brother and I were lying full-length, flat on our tummies on the upper bunks, watching fields, woods, lakes and rivers rush by. Cattle, people, boats, villages were so many dots or strange shapes rushing by almost too fast to be recognised. There was so much to see, near and far. By night it was wonderful to fall asleep to the puffing, clanking, screeching noises of the train.

When we came to the Urals, the world changed completely. No longer wide open vistas, we were enclosed, towered over and trapped. These were the first mountains I had seen and I did not like them. But I loved the beautiful collection of semi-precious stones, mined in the Urals, that Mother bought for me at a station. The case looked just like a large, thick book but it opened to reveal small compartments lined with cotton wool, with blue, yellow, purple or red stones in each. Rearranging the stones and learning their exotic names or just looking at them and admiring them was completely absorbing.

Beyond the Urals the country gradually flattened out and the only excitement was anticipating, stopping at and then departing from stations. Each time there was the fascinating climax of bustle as the train stopped, third-class passengers rushing to fill their kettles with hot water from the hot-water tap (no Russian travels without a kettle and small bags of tea and cube sugar), while the better-off ones could be seen sedately walking towards the station buffet to eat and drink and to buy various luxuries. Cheaper food by far was to be had from the peasant women who lined the remoter parts of the platform with their wares – butter and milk and *tvorog* (curd cheese), chicken and meats and fruit, spread out on neat, clean towels on the ground; and it all tasted so good.

Then there was the ritual of the station bell, all shining brass and prominently hung next to the buffet. It was rung three times before departure, each time creating near panic on the platform as people rushed to refill their kettles once more or to down their vodka in the buffet and to order another; and hurried to regain their seats. Meanwhile porters and guards closed the doors, the resplendently uniformed station-master majestically surveyed the scene and the whistle blew, the flag was waved and the train slowly glided away, then sped up. Platform and station and all its allurements were left behind and we were once again flying over the surface of the earth.

It took three weeks to Krasnoyarsk and the end of our journey. On the platform a number of men and women, immediately recognisable as political exiles, were waiting for the new arrivals. Newly arriving exiles were always eagerly awaited and warmly welcomed. On that very same platform some fifteen years earlier, the future Bolshevik leader Lenin had waited for his close friend and comrade Martov, the future Menshevik leader. Now we in our turn were at once surrounded and helped and escorted to the home of one of the exiles, where (it had already been decided) we were to lodge. Among political exiles in Siberia the grapevine worked perfectly: they always knew whom to expect and when and even what the newcomers would be bringing by way of books and journals, and letters from friends and relatives. And each time there was an air of celebration.

Krasnoyarsk was the residence of the governor of western Siberia and it was at his discretion that the place of exile in his region was allocated. After several days of waiting Mother was told that she was being sent to Kuragino, a village in the district of Minusinsk, not far from the village where Lenin had lived some fourteen years earlier. Both Lenin and we were lucky to be sent to that area, for it had an excellent climate. Had we been sent northwards we might well have landed, like so many exiles, in the terrible swamps of Turukhansk. That is what happened to Martov and it ruined his health.

We boarded a river steamer for Minusinsk, to spend five days and nights on the Yenisey River, so wide that at times when we were hugging one shore we could not see the other. Yet another adventure, another treat after the train. On the first day we were passing through the Krasnoyarsk Gorge, where the river narrows and is flanked by high red cliffs. It was a famous sight but I was too busy exploring our new abode to notice. There was such a lot to see and to do: climb the narrow, steep stairs from one deck to the next, marvel at the lifeboats and the high rolls of thick rope, peep through the port-hole and try the bunks in our cabin. I was not a bit sorry we were being exiled to Siberia!

On the third day the steamer came in view of a large island that looked as if it was capped by a high-domed white roof. It was in fact smothered by the white blossoms of *cheremukha* (bird-cherry tree). The heavy honey-sweet scent came in waves towards us. It was a marvellous sight. *Cheremukha* is a tall tree with heavy bunches of white flowers; I never saw it anywhere in western Europe but Russians love it and to my mind there is no other flowering tree, except perhaps acacia, to compare with it. We all ran to the railings, shouting with excitement while the boat slowed down and anchored just opposite the white island. The captain was persuaded to let us go ashore in small boats and wander about. Everybody grabbed as many branches as possible, whole armfuls. The ship's siren had sounded several times before we returned; we must have looked like a walking forest of flowers. The whole ship was decorated with the lovely white branches and the heavy scent hung over it all that day and night.

At the quay in Minusinsk there were again friends and comrades to welcome Mother; too many for me to know one from the other. And a few days later we were off again, in a horse-drawn carriage, for a day's drive to the village of Kuragino. There was only one political exile there but he had been warned to expect us and to rent a house for us. We entered the village through a barrier and found ourselves in a wide street. This was our first view of a Siberian village – prosperous, clean, wide-spaced. The houses were all of the same pattern: broad-fronted *izby* (log cabins) with large, ornately carved and gaily painted window frames and pots of bright red geraniums on the windows sills. The houses were separated from each other by wide, tall, solid wooden gates. And most of the houses had wooden benches in front.

When the local political exile was found he turned out to be a tall, lanky, very helpful young man and he had secured a whole *izba* for us. He showed us where it was, in the main and only street, helped us to carry our belongings inside and explained the arrangements. The house was furnished with simple but solid furniture and the kitchen was fully equipped; in the yard there was a small *izbushka* which was a bath-house and several outhouses and barns and sheds (for which we had no use). Right at the back of the yard there was even a small vegetable plot. It was a complete peasant homestead.

While Mother and the young man sat down at the table to talk, my brother and I rushed around exploring. By far the most interesting room was the kitchen. In most respects it was like any other Russian peasant kitchen, only cleaner and lighter. But then we had never before lived in a peasant house, so it was rather thrilling to have one of our own. One entered the house – up a few wooden steps and through a spacious porch – by the kitchen: a long room made to seem narrower than it really was by what looked like a high ledge along the whitewashed wall on the right. This ledge, about two-thirds of the height of the room, ran almost the entire length of the wall, ending in a baking oven at the other end of the kitchen. We recognised this as a traditional Russian *pech'* (stove). The long ledge was in fact a horizontal chimney through which the smoke and the heat travelled through the whole length of the kitchen before being expelled from the house. Thus when the oven was lit, it not only served to cook and to bake but also to heat the kitchen and even the next room. It was particularly cosy on top of the *pech'* where the old and the sick and the very young habitually slept.

This ingenious system of central heating always delighted Father, who was an engineer by training. He loved to point out that the Russian peasant, so often despised as being dirty and stupid, had several other clever mechanical devices which proved the opposite. There is, for instance, the *ruko-moynik* that supplied running water for washing. It is a cylinder, a little flattened on one side for hanging on the wall; it can be filled with water from above, while in its base there is a small round hole through which a tin stick protrudes. Looking inside the cylinder one can see that the stick has a flat, broad 'hat', like a mushroom, which in repose effectively seals the cylinder. When the stick is pushed up the water flows freely. A small stand with a china bowl under the *ruko-moynik* completes the arrangement. Father would say that the *pech'* and the *rukomoynik* were unappreciated abroad, while the samovar, much less ingenious and not unlike a Victorian tea urn, was undeservedly famous.

Well, we found the *pech'*, the samovar and the *rukomoynik*, a beautifully ornate one, in our kitchen, and escaping from the house we also found the *banya* (bath-house). This was a small log cabin with a narrow ante-room with a stove in it and a second, square, larger room with large wide vats for hot and cold water and deep wooden scoops for ladling the water out. In the corner of the room were the tiers for sweating; the higher one sat on these wooden benches, the hotter and steamier it was. Beyond the *banya* there were many other buildings to explore but at that point Mother called us in to help with the unpacking.

There was no lack of space in the house. We each had the luxury of a separate room and Mother had a large table for her study. The young man helped us to distribute our belongings and then showed us around. It turned out that my brother and I had overlooked the most delightful feature of the house: a trap door from the larder next to the kitchen led, down a steep ladder, into a large, very cold stone cellar with many shelves. On them stood intriguing bins and jars, some of earthenware, others of a strange and very attractive material unknown to us. The young man explained that these were made of birch bark and were a very typical Siberian kitchenware; they were called *krynki* and were used for storing milk, sour milk, cream, *tvorog* and butter, and were said to give these milk products a very agreeable aroma. But, alas, they were all empty and this reminded us that we were very hungry. 'Not to worry,' said the young man, for the land-lord, who lived in the house next to us, had asked us to eat with the family that evening. In the meantime the daughter of the house was bringing us some food. And sure enough, soon a pretty, rose-cheeked young girl in a bright embroi-dered blouse over a full, dark skirt did indeed arrive with milk and butter, freshly baked bread and *tvorog* and said that she would call for us in the late afternoon, 'when the men come back from the fields', to share their meal.

And what a meal it was! The large square deal table in the kitchen was set with plates and dishes of all kinds, all of them large and gay-patterned; and in the middle there was an even bigger open bowl filled to the brim with sour cream. But I had to contain my curiosity and my appetite, since we did not sit down to the meal straightaway. First we were welcomed by our hostess, a spare, neat elderly woman with quiet, dignified manners. The house, unlike ours, which seemed empty and spacious, was crowded with all kinds of objects. Our landlady explained that she had fifteen (or was it seven-teen?) children, and the house was only just big enough to hold them all. But then in Kuragino most families had twenty and more children. We were then shown the 'best room' where beds were piled high with embroidered covers and pillows and all kinds of cloths, and there were fine plates and bowls on embroidered tablecloths. This was not only a Siberian custom. Russian peasants' houses, or at least the more prosperous ones, also had a 'best room' where the best furniture and embroideries were kept, not for use but for show only, as testimony to the owners' prosperity.

At last the men came back from the fields; we saw the wide gates open and a caravan of carts, men and horses came into the yard. Passing by the house, they went on to the stables and barns, and having put away the carts and their contents and stabled the horses, made for the *banya*. Two of the younger boys came to the open kitchen window first, to collect from their mother a pile of towels and clean clothes. Now our hostess and her daughter busied themselves with filling the dishes on the table with butter and putting out the freshly baked bread and the *shangui*, a Siberian speciality this: flat buns with a topping of sour cream, which makes a delicious crust.

When the men came at last, clean and fresh after their bath, we were welcomed by our host in a dignified and friendly manner, and bid to sit down to the meal. I could hardly wait! The steaming hot bread loaves and the *shangui* were placed on the table, our host broke off a large chunk of bread and dipped it into the bowl of sour cream in the middle. Then, rather solemnly, he invited us all to do the same. There was a general eagerness to follow his example but there was no sign of greediness and no rush; everybody waited for us to take our turn. When the bowl was quite empty, it was removed and other food was set on the table. Our hostess urged us to taste this and that, but I had gorged myself on the delicious *shangui* and could not have eaten another bite. Mother remarked how tasty she found the bread and was told that it was baked every single day: 'Nobody in Siberia would dream of eating yesterday's stale bread.'

Our host spoke freely with Mother, and mentioned that he subscribed to newspapers; he was obviously very conscious that his style of living was far superior to that of Russian peasants. Whenever he alluded to Russian peasants, it was clear that he despised them for their ignorance and poverty. When we said goodbye and thanked them for the meal and the welcome and returned home, Mother commented on the visit. She explained that most Siberian peasants were descended from people, political convicts or else religious sectarians, who had been forcibly settled in Siberia. Hence the independent, defiant spirit, their dislike of the Russian authorities and their friendliness towards political exiles, 'state criminals' so-called. When settled on fertile land, as in the Minusinsk region, these settlers had usually prospered and acquired habits and manners very different from those of the downtrodden Russian peasantry.

I remember the summer in Kurangino as nearly idyllic. Mother was always there, either sharing our domestic chores and meals or working at her desk. She was translating a book (or was it articles?) by John Maynard Keynes and rushing to finish it, to be paid. This was indeed vital, as there was no way of earning anything in Kuragino and the state allowance for political prisoners was not enough to cover our rent. One day after I had been playing with some neighbours' children, I came home in a thoughtful mood. 'Mother,' I asked, 'Manya says I ought to be praying each night at bedtime, and thanking God for our daily bread.' But I was perplexed: 'Whom ought we to thank for our daily bread?' She laughed and said: 'Well, I suppose we ought to thank Maynard Keynes.' And that I did, so as not to be worsted by my playmate Manya. But this, my first religious phase, did not last long and I soon stopped praying.

Danya had meanwhile invented a new game. As usual he was the hero and I was cast in a minor role. As captain of an ocean-going ship – I being the cabin boy – he would rig up a kind of swing, using rotten cords slung over a crumbling old beam in the barn and a piece of rotten plank for a seat; we both stood on the seat and he gave several violent jerks to the swing until, invariably, disaster struck and either the seat or the beam or the cord or all three broke, leaving us to cling to whatever was left. Throughout the captain intoned in dramatic accents: 'we are on the high seas and the storm has broken . . . we round the tip of the land and there are dangerous cliffs ahead . . . and . . . oh! . . . yes . . . we have struck an underwater rock and the ship is going down . . . hold on, crew . . . oh! they are all thrown into the foaming waves and perish . . . and oh! . . . oh! . . . only I, the captain, am left and I must go down with my ship! . . . Oh! the brave captain . . .'

The cabin-boy, meanwhile, had been roughly flung on to the ground, had grazed her arms and legs and was not at all brave but snuffling and very eager to escape from any other disaster game. As always I was happier to play by myself, preferably in the ruined little house at the furthest end of the yard. It had long ago lost its roof and was open to the sky and the warm sun. Invaded by all kinds of flowering bushes and currant and raspberry canes, it had turned into a kind of green bower, where it was wonderful to sit and dream and be still and listen to the bees.

Sometimes I went with Mother to shop, first calling on some neighbours to buy fresh bread and various milk products and possibly a chicken, and then to stroll the whole length of the village street to the village store. This was always a treat. We walked along the wide street admiring the houses, all identical but for the differently painted and carved window frames and – a touch of luxury – pots of various bright flowers on the window sills. These pot plants were objects of great pride and also of rivalry among the women of the village; they were difficult to grow because of the short, very hot and dry summers and very long, cold winters. Sometimes we met the cattle being driven home from the fields and I remember that there was one particular, truly vicious cow which took great pleasure in kicking the flower pots off the sills. If she found a gate open she would enter the yard and wreak havoc there.

Occasionally we all three went for a walk outside the village, though we were warned not to stray too far because of the wild beasts and snakes which came down from the mountains. In early summer, the grasslands just outside the village were suddenly covered with wild flowers – mountain orchid, crocus and others. They grew in large, thick patches, transforming the meadows into patchworks of strong, bright colours, vivid against the backcloth of the Sayan mountains, which rose to the higher range of the Altay and ultimately to the Pamir, the Roof of the World. The Sayans were thickly covered by impenetrable forests, the taiga, where the brown bears roam and the black *razsomakha* cat watches from tree branches for its victims on the forest floor.

When the last harvest of the year had been brought in, the men of the village went out fishing or hunting and sometimes gold-washing. Gold-washing was done at the river's edge quite near the village, and all the children and young folk took part in it. A few shallow, wide metal pans and several large, fine sieves were needed, but the critical part was played by quicksilver. This was rented from an itinerant who visited the villages at that season, staying a few weeks in each. He arrived carrying all his belongings in a kind of rucksack, including his precious quicksilver in a strong little bottle. He rented it out, as I remember, for so much cash or for a share of the gold-dust. His arrival heralded a few exciting, festive weeks; the villagers were eager to make the best of his presence and worked long hours, as long, in fact, as daylight permitted. Gold-washing was an incredibly simple procedure: crouching at the very edge of the water one scooped some of the black gold-dust-carrying sand that ran like a snake on the river's edge. This was then 'washed' several times from pan to sieve and back again, until you could see the particles of gold gleaming in the remaining sand. At that stage the itinerant tipped his bottle and some of the quicksilver ran into the pan. The fine gold particles thereupon clustered around the globules of quicksilver while the sand fell away. I am a bit hazy about what followed – the excitement at that point reached its peak – but I think the globules with the gold-dust clinging to them were transferred to another, cleaner pan that was then warmed over a fire: the quicksilver liquefied and was poured off while the gold remained in the pan.

Siberian rivers are very rich in gold and our village usually washed considerable amounts of it during the few weeks' work. I cannot remember how it was divided among us all, but I know that all got a share, even my brother and I. I am sure that I took my small linen bag with gold back to Petrograd later on, but I cannot think what happened to it.

In autumn the men of the village and the older boys went into the mountains with large pots and many jars and bags of sugar to gather wild berries, which grew there in great abundance, to make jam on the spot. They usually camped in some convenient place as high as the horses and carts would go; then, leaving the younger boys in the camp, they would climb higher into the thickets of fruit bushes. All wore leather from head to toe and carried rifles as protection against snakes and wild beasts. In the evening they would return to the camp, light fires under the cast-iron pots and make jam. When all the jars were filled they returned to the village, women and children flocking to greet and cheer them as soon as the caravan was sighted. It was a joyful and festive occasion.

Imagine the thrill when my brother and his pal, our neighbour's son, were judged old enough to go with the men; and imagine how bubbling over with stories my brother was when he returned home. It was a bit disappointing, he said, to be left at the camp day after day when all the men and older boys left on their climb, but as he and his pal were allowed to pick from the raspberry bushes just outside the camp, as long as they did not stray further afield, it was not too bad. Well, said my brother, one day they went out to pick raspberries from a dense clump nearby. As they rounded the clump they separated until they could no longer see or even hear each other. For a little while there was silence and just the cracking of branches and the buzzing of insects above their heads, but then my brother saw a dark shape moving towards him from the other side of the bushes. Thinking it was his pal he hailed him but received no answer; he looked up and what he saw sent him racing to the camp – it was a bear, a big brown bear, erect on his hind legs, peacefully picking berries with both front paws and stuffing them into his mouth as fast as he could!

We could not stay in Kuragino, for Mother had no prospect of finding paid work there. So she applied for permission to move to the town of Minusinsk itself, and that was granted. In the autumn of 1915 we left Kuragino. During our drive there was one last glimpse of the wonders of that countryside. Our horse-drawn carriage had just emerged from a forest and we were skirting a big grassy field which at first sight seemed to be covered with little bumps. As we came out into the full sunlight the little bumps vanished. '*Susliki*,' said our coachman, 'friendly little fellows!' *Susliki* are marmots – and as we looked back we saw them re-emerging, one after another, hundreds of them, standing upright on their hind legs, heads all turned in our direction. How comic they seemed!

4

MINUSINSK WAS a small market town, dwarfed by the vast River Yenisey on which it stood. But it was a thriving little place. The administrative centre of an enormous region, it was equipped with banks, commercial offices, hospitals and schools. Political exiles were able to find jobs in all of these. And political exiles were numerous, in fact they formed a large and colourful colony. Political disagreements faded in exile, to be replaced by solidarity and mutual respect. All ages and all shades of dissent were represented, from Anarchists and Social Revolutionaries to Bolsheviks and Mensheviks. Some were exiled for life, others for many years, others again had already many years of exile behind them.

Mother often took me to visit the most celebrated of all the exiles, Yekaterina Breshko-Breshkovskaya. A living legend, she was venerated far beyond her own *Narodniki* (Populist) Party. She had been born into a family of prosperous landed gentry and had married into the same class. In the 1860s, she and her husband had enthusiastically supported the government-sponsored movement for rural development; but tiring of the slow and frustrating work of founding and running village schools, hospitals and dispensaries, she had left her husband to join the clandestine revolutionary movement. Repeatedly arrested, she became the first woman to be sentenced to hard labour in the Siberian gold mines. Now she was once again in Siberian exile. When I met her she was a grey-haired old lady with humorous eyes and a spirit as indomitable as ever. In 1917 she was to be hailed as 'the grandmother of the Revolution'.

We soon settled down in this new environment. Mother had the luck to be put in charge of the town dispensary; this was a well-paid job, and moreover it carried with it a large flat on the top floor of the dispensary. My brother had to return to his school in St Petersburg – now renamed, for patriotic reasons, Petrograd – so Mother and I were left on our own. Mother found her job rather demanding, and often she was on night duty. However, she could now afford a maid, and soon buxom, red-cheeked Marfa joined our household. Cheerful and often boisterous, she could at times be unexpectedly reposeful – notably when we sat together on the bench in front of the house, sunning ourselves, while she chewed cedar-gum. Round and round went her mouth and round and round went her eyes, as they took in everything there was to see in the street. In the kitchen she was all energy, absolutely tireless, as she baked sheets of flat cedar-nut cakes, or else rolled out yard upon yard of noodle pastry for *pel'meni*, small pasties filled with meat which were the staple Siberian food.

My days were mostly spent with the Dan family. Politically and personally the Dans were very close to Mother. Fyodr Ilyich Dan, who was a medical doctor by profession and currently head of one of the two Minusinsk hospitals, was a leading Menshevik. Lydia Osipovna Dan belonged to the famous Zederbaum family. Her eldest brother, Yuly Osipovich Zederbaum, adopted the name Martov – just as Vladimir Ilyich Ulyanov adopted the name Lenin. Her other two brothers, Sergey and Vladimir, were also well-known Mensheviks. Of the three sisters, Lydia was the only one to become an active revolutionary. Though not beautiful, she possessed a unique charm which captivated all who knew her. She readily undertook the task of giving me lessons, along with her own daughter Missya. Her lively manner and her sense of fun made learning easy and we were both very willing pupils. After lessons I almost always stayed for lunch and then played with Missya until Mother or Marfa collected me.

Missya, thin as a matchstick, with sharp little eyes and quick darting movements, not at all pretty but very bright, had a magnetic quality and a kind of spiritual authority which fascinated even grown-ups. Once the prominent Menshevik Irakly Tsereteli came to stay for a few days with the Dans. Tsereteli, who was in exile in Irkutsk, had come to get the exiles in Minusinsk to sign an anti-war declaration, which became known as the 'Declaration of Siberian Internationalists'. This tall and very handsome Georgian, later to become a minister in the coalition government of 1917, was unmarried and generally ignored children. But when Missya made fun of him he got really angry. Lydia Osipovna tried to placate him: 'How can you let her get under your skin, she is only a child!', and he would say: 'She's not a child, she's a witch!'

I, by contrast to Missya, was a somewhat plump little eight-year-old with slow movements and sleepy eyes and she soon had me under her spell. In our games, mostly of Missya's invention, I followed her into a magic world of make-believe, in which we enacted, without any kind of props, whole dramas. We would spend many hours crouching behind bushes, whispering to each other, breathless with excitement or fear, our minds inventing dangers and catastrophes. Although Missya was a great tyrant and ordered me about a lot, she also made it clear that I was the first to have been admitted into her world of imaginings and that she considered me a very special friend. She was my first real playmate, my first real friend, and I was utterly happy. But soon the winter set in and the Dans were transferred to another place, on the River Angara, near Irkutsk. I was grief-stricken at losing Missya. I did not know then that I was losing her forever; she died two years later of meningitis.

The departure of the Dans left me without a playmate. Once again I had to play by myself. I realised now that my games were much less inventive and dramatic than Missya's or even Danya's, but I liked my own potterings, my own quiet world of baby baths and kitchen sinks – all in the mind, invisible to the onlooker. I shook out imaginary bedding, turned on imaginary taps, cooked imaginary meals – unexciting and tame by comparison, but allowing much more room for feeling. And even though they lacked variety, these games never bored me.

Soon I acquired a new friend, or even two: a boy called Pavel and his Irish Setter Bea. Pavel was the son of a Bolshevik exile who was the director of the town hospital in Minusinsk (Dan had been the director of the district hospital). As I understood it, Pavel's mother was a concert pianist in Moscow and could not or did not choose to follow her husband into exile. 'A house without a woman is not a home,' said Mother, and I remember the gloomy impression it made on us when we went to see them. Both father and son looked gloomy too, though both were very good-looking. Mother extended a standing invitation and it soon became evident that Alexander Pavlovich much preferred dining with us to dining at home. In spite of their political differences, he and Mother became great friends and he was an almost daily visitor. As for Pavel, he came to us every day after school and our Marfa fed him and washed and mended his clothes. She also spread a blanket for Bea in a corner of the kitchen and that beautiful (and faithless, said Pavel) animal installed herself there as a permanent fixture.

We took to going on long walks outside the town, Pavel and I and Bea. Only the very centre of Minusinsk, the market place and a few streets leading out of it made it look like a town; a little way out it was nothing but a sprawling village. One could get out of it in no time at all. And then one was in the steppe. The beauty of those limitless grasslands under limitless skies was breathtaking. Stopping at the edge of the steppe we could see the tall steppe grass, *kovyl'*, reel and weave in the wind, changing colour from creamy grey to silver as it moved. It was like standing on the shore of the sea.

There was an unbroken view to the very horizon, punctuated only by small hillocks here and there – the burial mounds, *kurgany*. Sometimes, as we stood still, spellbound, a rider on a small fast horse would shoot across the steppe like a black arrow.

These were the homelands of the Abakan Tartars, a nomadic Turkic tribe, who wandered with their herds of horses from winter pastures to summer pastures and back again. When they settled in the Abakan valley, they lived in clusters of yurts. Pavel's father, who was sometimes summoned to attend a sick elder, said that it was very cosy inside a yurt, the floors and walls being covered with hand-woven carpets. And half-way up, shelves all around the yurt carried a quantity of round-bellied pots used for mares' milk; the wealth of the owners was measured by the number of these mare-milk pots. We saw many of the pots, and many gold ornaments, when we went to the Minusinsk Museum, which had been established by a political exile of an earlier generation. There were also life-size figures of the shamans with all the tools of their calling. They seemed so alive!

Other Siberian nomad tribes such as the Kirghiz also lived near Minusinsk. On market days whole cavalcades of these fascinating people rode into town, all dressed in long, black velvet kaftans, the women wearing long earrings of gold coins that often hung down to their waists – also a measure of wealth. I loved their flat faces, slit eyes, jet black hair. They were reserved and dignified, with a kind of concentrated stillness in their bodies and faces. When in town the men were a bit wary, and their movements were slow, but they were galvanised into intense energy when they left it. Then they let their black horses streak across the steppe while the women followed more slowly clutching their purchases.

I thoroughly enjoyed market days in Minusinsk. It was then that my life-long addiction to markets took hold of me. Mother would take me with her to help choose and then carry the food. There were stalls for meat, poultry and dairy produce, while vegetables and fruit, particularly melons and water melons, were laid out on the ground, in heaps. Everything was sold in what appeared to us huge quantities. When mother asked the butcher for a piece of beef for roasting, of about three to four pounds in weight, he looked at her in pitying silence for a few seconds and then explained that no roast could have its full flavour under ten to fifteen pounds – surely she ought to know that? We compromised on six pounds and found the roast, hot or cold, delicious.

Buying a water melon was quite a ritual. First you walked slowly among the heaps, appraising their general look. There was a bewildering variety of them – oblong or round, small or large, dark green all over or only in stripes, or blotched in two tones of green. Having chosen your heap you asked the vendor for 'a taste', and he cut out a large triangle from one of the sort you fancied, and you tasted it, carefully and slowly. If you did not like it or found it not sweet enough, you could ask to taste several others, before making the final purchase. Most locals bought several melons as well as water melons at a time. As we carried our purchases home, Mother often spoke of the contrast between this abundance and the hunger which was raging in wartime Russia.

Skirting the stall and the market proper, trappers and hunters and gold-washers, on foot and on horseback, made first for the town bank and the large warehouses there, to sell their hides and furs and bags of gold-dust or nuggets washed from the mountain rivers. Then they moved on to buy equipment and groceries in the shops that lined the market square. Sometimes a whole troop came riding in, Tartars or hunters from the Sayan mountains. In autumn peasants brought cart-fuls of cedar nuts to the market – a great Siberian delicacy. In winter, milk in the market was sold in large, flat frozen discs and we carried several of these home to be broken into pieces and melted. But, of course, it was also great fun to suck a piece of frozen rich Siberian milk; it was as good as ice cream.

In winter the market shrank to just a few stalls, the roads were covered with snow and the Tartars no longer came riding into the market square. Sledges, harnessed to one, two or three horses, took over from the horse carts of summer. Snow blizzards buffeted the town and heaped the snow into untidy drifts in the streets. The river was iced over and formed now the only road to Krasnoyarsk. And in the houses the 'Dutch' stoves were lit.

These stoves were dangerous. Once the coal was properly glowing a stove had to be hermetically closed, as the least crack which allowed the carbon monoxide to escape would cause poisoning. Mother and I soon found out what happened then. Marfa had lit the stove in the bath house for us, and when we arrived it was beautifully warm and the water was steaming in a large vat. We sat down on the bench that ran along the side of the wall and began to soap and rub ourselves, but after a while I began to feel sleepy, and so did Mother. It would have been so easy to sit back and go to sleep, and to die in our sleep! But Mother suddenly realised what was happening. Grasping me by the hand she staggered out of the door and then through the outer door, and we fell naked into the deep snow and rolled in it until the sleepiness cleared. Then I felt very ill indeed.

Mother was an excellent cook, like her mother before her, and her dinners were welcomed as pleasant distractions in the drab life of the exiles in Minusinsk. I was intensely interested in the preparations for these dinners and in the events themselves. With Marfa's help Mother concocted innumerable *zakuski* (starters), cold and hot, as well as main dishes, and I would sit at the large kitchen table and watch, and sometimes help, chopping and mixing or whatever. Then, in the evening, I was allowed to sleep in the room next to the one in which the dinner would take place. As the guests assembled, some ten to twelve men (I do not remember any women), tiptoed through my darkened room, and when the door closed on the last of them, I stopped pretending to be asleep, propped myself up against my pillows and prepared to listen and to guess what was happening behind that closed door.

I knew that they would first help themselves to the *zakuski*, which were set out on the round table next to the door. The plates clanked, the forks jingled, and I heard them exclaim, as they helped themselves, 'Excellent fish!', 'What a pâté!', 'Ah, a *zapekanka*, my favourite!' And then the chair legs scraped on the floor and the voices moved away a little, as everyone settled down at the long dinner-table drawn into the middle of the room. I knew them all; they were mostly my mother's Menshevik comrades, though Pavel's Bolshevik father was also usually there.

Conversation stopped as the glasses were filled. Then Mother's voice: 'Friends, note the variety of my own *nalivki* – they have matured nicely.' She had prepared them herself: putting lemon rind or various other fruit at the bottom of bottles, filling them up with alcohol and then putting the bottles between the panes of the double windows to mature. There were many, many windows in our flat and in each of these there were two or even four bottles; they changed colour as the *nalivka* matured, and the colours were like precious stones in the sun. Now these bottles would be standing on the table and the guests would be sampling the various liqueurs, holding them up to the light and smacking their lips. I could almost see them.

Between the *zakuski* and the hot dishes brought in by Marfa I sometimes went to sleep; the talk became slow and measured and was usually about politics, and I soon became bored. But sometime later I would wake up to very different sounds: laughter and singing and the strumming of a guitar and the stamping of feet. They must have finished eating, though not drinking – I could still hear the glasses clink. I could imagine the guitarist sitting a little away from the table; this was Yermolaev, a friendly looking man with a curly head of hair and a quiet smile always on his lips. And the singer was Ikov, a very different man, restless and nervy, his face all profile and his movements jerky as he ceaselessly moved around the table and around the room. But his voice went straight to one's heart and I could listen to him by the hour. I learned all my Siberian songs from Ikov. My favourites were the two songs about escaped convicts: one about the fugitive crossing Lake Baykal on an upturned fish-barrel for a boat with a torn shirt for a sail, the other about the convict crossing the lake singing a plaintive song of his native land. These songs always reduced the whole company to a long silence, while I wept desperately into my pillow.

As if to throw off the sadness, somebody proposed a game – the favourite game of Siberian exiles, the Travelling Game. Invariably there would be a lengthy argument about which section of the railway line they should choose to travel on. Well, the stretch best known to them all was from Chelyabinsk to Krasnoyarsk, so they usually agreed on that. Before the game began I could hear Mother removing plates and dishes to the side table and putting more bottles out. And then one of the men called out with a booming 'official' voice: 'Chelyabinsk station; train will be departing in three minutes: gentlemen, fill your glasses!' There was some noise as the chairs were pushed back and glug-glug as the drinks were poured out. And then the chorus of voices: 'Bing-bong, bing-bong, first bell! Gentlemen, down your drinks!' I remembered so vividly the stops on our journey to Siberia: the station bell, the buffet and the counter where one got the drinks, and then, after the third bell, the rush of the passengers back to their carriages. I could hear them downing their glasses next door and then: 'Gentlemen, refill your glasses!' and again, 'Bing-bong, bing-bong, second bell! Gentlemen, down your drinks!' – sounds of downing, again, 'Gentlemen, refill your glasses!' – chorus of 'Bing-bong, bing-bong, third bell! Gentlemen, down your drinks' etc., and then the 'official voice': 'The train is about to depart from Chelyabinsk'. Laughter and then a chorus of 'Chug-chug, chug-chug, chug-chug', sometimes blurred somewhat with the munching and crunching of savoury titbits. The company became more subdued, less noisy, though soon they got into an argument about which

[69]

station came next. Once they agreed on that, the routine of
the three bells and the drinks was resumed. And so on and so
on. I don't remember how many times it was repeated, but
long before they got half-way to Krasnoyarsk, the tempo
slackened, voices got thick and slurred, there was some
snoring and, unmistakably, Ikov was sobbing.

At that point Mother usually intervened: 'All the food is
eaten, and all the drink is drunk and it's time for everyone to
go home.' She alone was still sober. It took a long time for
everybody to say goodbye and thank you. At last the door
opened and in the shaft of light from the next room, I could
see their huddled figures swaying and stumbling across my
room. I dived under my covers, peeping out to watch Marfa
and Mother guiding unwilling arms and feet into coat sleeves
and galoshes, crowning heads with their headgear, and gently
propelling everyone through the outer door. 'Goodnight!
Goodnight!' And I could hear Mother sigh sadly on the way
to her late bed. She glanced suspiciously at me but I pre-
tended to be fast asleep.

It must have been early in 1916 that we received news of my
half-sister Galya's illness. Mother at once applied for permission to go to her but she was refused and Galya soon died of
meningitis. I never saw Mother so shattered. She did not
speak of it, did not share her grief with me, went about her
work as usual, and I could only guess at her thoughts and
feelings. Did she blame herself for having chosen a way of
life that often took her away from her children, even when
they needed her most? I suspected that she did, though I also
thought that nothing would make her leave her chosen path.

I sympathised; since our arrival in Minusinsk I had acquired a romantic admiration for political exiles, for their heroism, their suffering, their steadfastness. I thought it right that Mother should be just like the best of them. I think it was about then that I began to worship Revolution as a kind of deity, to which all private concerns had to be sub-ordinated. Certainly I did not blame Mother for Galya's death. But my half-sister Sanya did.

When Sanya and, somewhat later, the rest of the family – Danya, Father and Grandmother Sara – arrived in Minusinsk, Sanya was full of resentment against Mother. She declared that she hated all Mensheviks, and went out of her way to make friends with Bolsheviks among the exiles, espe-cially with Yelena Stasova, a prominent member of the Bolshevik Central Committee. She even became engaged to the Bolshevik Anton Adasinsky. He was a quiet, kindly man, several years older than she was, who had been exiled for life. Sanya was then nineteen and was going back to Petrograd to continue her education, so our parents, convinced that she was simply acting out her spite against Mother, took little notice of her marriage plans. They were proved wrong, for she did eventually marry Anton. The marriage proved very successful, and Sanya became a convinced Bolshevik. Nobody could have foreseen that in Stalin's purge of the Communist Party in the 1930s Anton would be shot and Sanya and her daughter sent to a labour camp for many years.

All this lay in the future. In the meanwhile Sanya worked off much of her bitterness in strenuous physical pursuits. One of her favourite occupations was snake hunting. Armed with only a long, sturdy stick, she would walk out of town, always by herself. Among the large, flat stone slabs left over from an old quarry, there lived many snakes, particularly the ugly black local snake, which was very poisonous. Sanya would position herself atop these stone slabs, having collected several smaller stones, and wait for the snakes to crawl to the surface. Then, with one swift throw she would crush a snake's head and then prod the still quivering victim with her long stick. Incredibly the 'dead' snake would wind itself firmly around the stick and hold on to it for a long time. Several hours later, Sanya would return to the town, walking always in the middle of the street and whistling jauntily, her stout stick carried over her shoulder with some five or seven snakes dangling from it. She was usually accompanied by quite a few local boys – a conquering heroine returning home. I had always been scared of snakes and went into hysterics each time Sanya deliberately spread out her trophies in the living-room. Fortunately Mother, who had been unusually gentle and forbearing with Sanya, firmly told her to remove them. But Sanya had the last word; she threw the dead snakes down the lavatory, incidentally causing me acute constipation!

Though she had a grudge against me, 'Mother's pet', she had a generous nature. She even saved my life once. We had gone by boat to 'the island', a favourite place for outings – a largish island across a narrow channel of the Yenisey, just across from Minusinsk. It was a green island with a dense forest at one end and fields with cattle here and there. We were Sanya, Danya, me and a young student. It was a beautiful, hot day and we looked for shade and a tree to tie the boat to. We found a lovely place where the shore was lined with willows, their branches overhanging the water. The boat was made fast, the basket with food was passed from hand to hand and then deposited on the grass. We were all standing in the boat preparing to step ashore. The boat was swaying as first the student and Danya and then Sanya jumped off. I was unsteady on my feet and the next thing I knew was that I had overbalanced and fallen overboard.

It all happened so quickly, I had no time to be frightened. I was gently floating and turning in an opaque green space, a kind of liquid chamber of translucent ripples and bubbles, with gold flecks where the sunbeams struck. It was all very beautiful and I felt blissfully content. I don't know how long I floated, but suddenly there was a sharp tug and I was brutally hoisted up. Later I was told that as soon as Sanya realised I had fallen into the river, she raced forward to overtake the current, climbed on to one of the willow branches, crawled to the very end of it and stretched herself full-length on the branch, with one arm laid along the branch and the other dangling over the water. I had come up twice already, but on the third time she grabbed me by the hair and hauled me out. When we both lay panting on the warm grass, we saw that one of Sanya's arms was lacerated and bleeding from wrist to armpit. But she brushed our concern aside and applied herself to reviving me. Only when I was stripped of my wet clothes and wrapped in the student's shirt did she allow us to wind the picnic tablecloth round her arm. Then the food was unpacked and we all discovered that we were ravenously hungry and we all talked at once, very companionably and very pleased with each other.

My last memory of Minusinsk is of one very special occasion after Father, Danya and Sanya had all left for Petrograd. The winter was well advanced, and land and river were covered with thick snow and ice, when Mother took me one night for a sledge ride. The troika called for us as dusk was falling. The inside of the sledge was covered with thick reindeer hides, and the coachman had brought thick reindeer coats, hide outside and fur inside. With Marfa's help he put these coats on top of our own coats, then wound yards and yards of cloth round us. Enormous fur mittens and hats completed the robing. Finally we were lifted on to the sledge and tucked into a thick fur rug, so that only our noses remained uncovered.

By that time it was quite dark. The sledge slid soundlessly down the snow-covered street, across the white and empty market place and down a slope on to the frozen surface of the river. The coachman had taken the descent gently and carefully, but now he sprang the troika and we flew through the milky air, hardly, it seemed to me, touching the earth. The snow under the sledge felt firm – no doubt pressed down by the many sledges that had already travelled this way that winter – but on both sides snow lay in high, loose banks. The sky was low and as grey-white as the earth and we seemed to be driving in an unlit tunnel. But then the moon rose and the tunnel seemed to broaden and the walls to roll back. The sky lifted and grew brighter and there were stars; and the snow below glittered and sparkled with myriads of tiny lights, while we flew half-way between the earth and the sky. It was unbelievably and overwhelmingly beautiful.

5

It was still winter when the news of the (February) Revolution reached us. I had grown up with that word; from my earliest days I had been taught to expect that universal festival, that fulfilment of all hopes. The REVOLUTION! My parents had lived for it; all their friends had lived for it; they had all been ready to die for it. I imagined it as something unspeakably glorious and wonderful. And now it had come!

Even in Minusinsk, so remote from the hub of events, life changed overnight. The local policemen disappeared and the exiles amused themselves by looking for their personal folders in the files of the police station. It emerged that each one had been given a nickname: Mother was described as *Surovaya* (the stern one). Everybody longed to get back to Russia to take part in these exciting events; everybody wanted to leave as soon as possible, or almost everybody. For a few the news of the Revolution had come too late: one 'lifer', unable to readjust, shot himself.

The general desire to leave Minusinsk at once met with two obstacles. The ice on the Yenisey was expected to start cracking any day, and then the frozen road would become unsafe. Also the townspeople objected to the sudden departure of all the professionals. At a hastily convened general meeting at the town hall, the mayor was in tears: 'Siberia has been a mother to you, yet you are leaving us without a thought for the hospital, the pharmacy, the school, the bank. They will have no staff and will have to close . . . What will become of us?' So it was decided that departures should be staggered, so as to permit at least partial replacement of key personnel. And by general agreement Yekaterina Breshko-Breshkovskaya was to be the first to leave. There was a festive send-off for the old lady. Speeches were made and the word Revolution came into all of them. I liked to listen and to see everybody so happy and jolly, quite unlike their former selves. But I felt very puzzled. No doubt, I thought, I will get to know what it is all about when we ourselves return to Petrograd.

By the time Mother and I could leave, travelling had become highly dangerous. There were visible cracks in the ice of the river, some as thin as pencil-marks, others broader. Any day now, everybody said, the ice would begin to move. Our journey would take us several days and nights along the river, until we hit the overland road to the railway line. We could, of course, wait for the steamer, but that was months away. So Mother decided to leave at once and chance it. We set off in a wide travelling sledge padded with many fur rugs and harnessed to a troika. Before we set out we were warned by experienced travellers of two major risks: the ice might indeed begin to move, in which case the coachman was to make for the nearest shore at once. Also there were packs of wolves roaming the countryside. It would seem that years of war had deprived the countryside of marksmen who usually kept the packs at bay and the wolves had become more daring, approaching villages and attacking travellers and horses. Mother was advised to carry a piglet or two in the back of the sledge and feed them to the wolves if necessary. She absolutely refused to follow this advice and took a rifle instead.

Smothered in fur coats, rugs, scarves, hats and gloves we were snug, lying full-length in the sledge which glided smoothly over the deep snow. But we could not sleep. In some places wind had swept the ice clean and we could see the ominous pencil-marks. Now and then a deep groan sounded from below and the coachman urged the horses to go faster: 'The ice, lady, is groaning to get free ...' And indeed twice we got into an area of cracked ice; once our troika actually broke through and we had to pull it out. We were relieved when we could leave the river for firm land. But now the dread of wolves kept us awake. We saw no sign of them during the day, but days were short, and as soon as dusk fell, wolves' eyes, like points of light, shone in the dark. Then the horses began to snort and lay their ears back and roll their eyes in a frenzy of fear. Mother turned over and held the rifle at the ready. In our loneliness and helplessness, we watched desperately for another kind of light to appear, the welcoming lights of a village. The grey-white snowy wilderness seemed to close over us, cutting us off from all help.

But we were lucky: on all three occasions that we were chased by wolves, we reached a village before they reached us. It was such a relief to enter the safe haven of the posting-inn. There we were helped out of our wrappings, put in front of hot stoves to dry and warm ourselves, given delicious hot *shanga* and plates of steaming soup with chunks of meat in it. All the while the samovar hummed and sang on the table and the hot tea was fragrant with honey. The round white globe of the oil lamp suspended from the ceiling above the table threw a strange light on people's faces and on the portraits of bearded generals on the walls. And then the beds, piled up high with pillows and padded blankets, in which one sank straight away into the deepest sleep. In the morning there was hot gruel and more sweet tea and a new coachman with fresh horses, which seemed to go twice as fast as the tired team of the night before.

When we finally got to the railway station — it was the major junction at Chelyabinsk — we were suddenly surrounded by people, crowds of them. After our lonely journey, it seemed another world. I remember dimly that Mother was repeatedly addressing crowds of people and that we were meeting many of our Petrograd friends, who were, like us, returning home from Siberian exile. Mother seemed to be shaking hands with somebody every minute, while I kept as close to her skirts as possible for fear of getting lost. Then, suddenly, we were in Petrograd.

Mother was fretting, deeply frustrated, I could feel, that she had not been in the thick of things when they happened. She plunged immediately into frantic activity. Elected to the Central Committee of the Menshevik Party, she quickly rose to the important position of Secretary.

As for Father, he had been in the thick of things all along. While Mother, as an Internationalist, had been exiled to Siberia, he, with other Defensists, had been helping the war effort. He had even helped to found the Workers' Group, which was affiliated to a non-party organisation called the War Industry Committee. But by the beginning of 1917 the situation had changed. Catastrophic defeats in battle, massive casualties, hunger spreading throughout the land, an ever more widespread recognition that the conduct of the war was being ruined by incompetence and corruption in high places – all this together had produced a general disaffection. The Workers' Group was not immune, and the government responded by arresting the whole group, including Father.

From the windows of their cells in the centre of Petrograd the prisoners saw workers streaming along the streets, calling for bread and peace. On the very next morning the crowds broke into the prison. This was the beginning of the February Revolution. Father and his comrades were carried shoulder-high to the Tauride Palace, where the Duma was in session. There the Petrograd Soviet of Workers' and Soldiers' Deputies was created. Once again soviets were a Menshevik initiative, as they had been in 1905; whereas in 1905 the soviets had been easily suppressed by the government, this time the enterprise struck root. The Petrograd Soviet had mass support. Father was at once elected to the executive and to the secretariat of this new body.

Events moved with astonishing speed. A provisional government was formed, the Tsar abdicated, and my parents were busier than ever. Neither of them was much at home. Mother was completely taken up with party work, while Father hardly ever left the Tauride Palace, where the Soviet was in permanent session: he even spent the nights there, snatching short naps on some sofa or on a blanket on the floor. But where did this leave me? Washed up on a lonely beach, all alone – that is what it felt like. And with not a clue as to what was happening. If only the family meals had continued, with at least one parent present and guests coming and going, I would have gleaned from the table-talk what was going on: I was after all nine years old. But there was nothing of that kind, only an empty flat and the three of us: Danya and me, with a grudging Sanya in charge. Not even Grandmother Sara was with us; she was away visiting her own family in Svenciany.

We were living in a working-class district near the Obvodny Canal, surroundings much less attractive than our previous family home on the other side of the Neva. Sanya and Danya were both out by day: he at school and she working at some co-operative. Eventually I, too, was sent to school. I hated it. I was not used to school routine and found it difficult to take. Teachers fussed over my lack of previous schooling and the pupils bullied me because I did not fit in and because my hair was carroty red. I was wearing a green corduroy coat lined throughout with white lamb; I loved that coat and was very proud of it but because of its colour they shouted 'spinach and egg' after me. I was utterly miserable.

After the plenty of Minusinsk, I could not get used to the dearth of everything in Petrograd. I was miserably cold at school and at home because fuel was rationed and in short supply. The larder was bare for the same reasons. The only thing to do was to go to bed, pile everything available on top of me and find oblivion in a book. Probably it was then, half-frozen and half-starved, that I became addicted to reading.

Ever since, I have been able to forget the world for the printed page.

I forget why and when I stopped going to school and took to the streets. I had legitimate reasons to be there: I was told to get our food rations, which meant waiting in endless queues at the local food store. I also went to the local open-air market on the canal quay, where I rarely managed to get anything for the larder, but which I loved. The streets adjoining the market were drab but full of people. And it was here that I got my own personal experience of revolutionary crowds – not storming palaces or building barricades, but gathering peacefully at street corners for a chat or an argument, everybody everybody's friend. I never understood how it came about that a few people somehow became a group and several groups grew into a crowd and indeed into a political meeting. A worker, a student, possibly a soldier or sailor, would jump up on a box or whatever was handy, and would begin a speech. Words like 'revolution . . . our soviet . . . up with . . . down with . . . we demand . .. insist . . . reject . . .' pattered down on our heads like beans spilling from an upturned bucket. Sometimes a lad would be dispatched to the Tauride Palace to fetch a 'live' soviet deputy and he would arrive to address the meeting. The crowd listened and cheered and heaved with approval or disapproval. I could rarely follow the gist of the speeches but I felt myself part of the crowd, sharing that special warmth that a happy Russian crowd generates. Those were the spring days of the Revolution and there I found elation and joy.

With the coming of summer the scene and the mood seemed to change. For one thing, food was not getting any more plentiful; for another, people were unhappy about the new government and the continuing war. We were no longer living near the Obvodny Canal. I have no idea what happened to Sanya and Danya, but I was living with Mother somewhere else. That is, I was not exactly living with her – most days I was dumped with whatever Menshevik family had children of my age, while Mother rushed away on party business. I remember best of all the Chkheidzes. Their father, a Georgian Menshevik, was chairman of the Petrograd Soviet and was seldom at home. Mrs Chkheidze was a busy but friendly woman and made me welcome; the children and I were allowed to play in their father's study, where the bulky leather-covered chairs and sofa, overturned, made perfect trains, tunnels and boats. Another family where I was occasionally dumped was that of Martov's brother Sergey and his wife Konkordia. Both were prominent Mensheviks and there was much coming and going at their house. Konkordia Ivanovna had a very special gift of drawing people out, me included, and I was happy talking to her, and happy to be there. There was just one difficulty: Martov's sister, our old friend Lydia Dan, was likely to drop in on them any time and she could not bear to see me as I reminded her of her dead daughter Missya. So I had to be spirited away as soon as she arrived. Eventually, she asked to see me and we met and talked for a while. So began a close and lifelong friendship.

There were two visits of a very different kind that we made. Mother took me to see the two legendary Veras, Vera Figner and Vera Zasulich. Both were famous for their revolutionary past; Vera Figner had spent twenty years in the fortress prison of Shlusselburg, on an island in the Gulf of Finland. She had gone to her cell as a young woman and a very beautiful one. She was now an old woman with a lined but still very beautiful face, of the same kind of icon-like frozen beauty as Anna Akhmatova. And inwardly, too, she seemed frozen. Loneliness had become second nature to her; she lived in it as in a cocoon and could not, or would not, come out of it. Her manner was friendly and she asked Mother a lot of questions about the political situation, yet she seemed to be miles away, perhaps back in her fortress cell.

Vera Zasulich was very different. A lumpy, untidy old woman, she was mentally extraordinarily alert and full of interest in contemporary events. As a young woman she had shot and wounded the police chief of St Petersburg in revenge for his arbitrary and cruel treatment of fellow revolutionaries then on trial. Fortunately for her a legal reform was introduced, and she herself was tried in one of the first trials by jury held in Russia – and was acquitted. Before she could be rearrested, she was smuggled abroad. She stayed there for many years. She turned her back on terrorism and became, with Lenin, Martov, Axelrod and Plekhanov, one of the founders of the Russian Social Democratic Workers' Party and of *Iskra*. It was during these *Iskra* years that Mother met her in Switzerland, and even stayed with her in the nightmarish room in which Vera Zasulich lived, wrote for and edited the paper. The whole floor and Vera's narrow cot were covered mountain high with newspapers and galleys, and when Mother was asked to stay the night, she slept on top of stacks of newspapers on the floor. In the morning they shared a breakfast cooked on a Bunsen burner! Now in her old age Vera's talk was still fascinating, her questions astute and to the point. She lived, like the other Vera, in a room in a hospice provided by the State and she found it empty and impersonal; she was not used to being on the sidelines. She fretted and fumed about Lenin and his Bolsheviks; she and her fellow Iskrist Axelrod sided with the Mensheviks.

Mother obviously admired both women tremendously, but in very different ways. Vera Figner represented the heroic past of the revolutionary movement and the initial inspiration of Mother's whole life, while Vera Zasulich belonged to the present. It occurs to me as I write that Mother must have named me Vera after one of them – Vera (Faith, in Russian) is such an unsuitable name for a Jewish child!

Some incidents that took place during these early days of the Revolution I cannot date at all. When was it that we went to hear Chaliapin in the Narodny Dom (House of the People) sing a mixed programme of opera arias and revolutionary songs such as 'Akh, *dubinushka, ukhnem. . .*', his huge voice booming out to fill that colossal hall? And when and where did we see pre-revolutionary Russian films: heavily romantic love stories played by stars like Ivan Mozhukhin and Vera Kholodnaya? And when was it that Mother and I went to stay with friends in an apartment on the fifth floor of a house on the corner of the Nevsky and the Liteyny Prospekts, the two busiest and most important streets in town? That was an experience! All day and most of the night, military lorries thundered down the Nevsky and by day overcrowded trams clink-clanked along the Liteyny. Crowds of people moved up and down both streets, overflowing on to the pavement. The lovely parquet flooring of the Nevsky was ankle deep in mud and slush. But the scene was lent a festive air by the broad strips of scarlet cloth stretched from rooftop to rooftop. Printed on them, black on red, were political slogans or lines from Mayakovsky's poetry. When it was not too cold, I loved to sit on the highest of the steps in front of the house, watching and listening. The two currents of people moving in both directions, the stray phrases caught from passers-by, the honking of the lorries and the ding-dong of the trams – it all fused for me into an exhilarating sense of living, of partaking in the life of the city.

I seem to remember that the two children of the family were not allowed to go out by themselves; they were altogether 'too well brought up' for my taste and they must have found me pretty wild. The only enjoyable occasions shared with them were the visits of Korney Chukovsky, whose books for children were read and loved by everybody in Russia. When he came to visit, we three children waylaid him in the hall and got him to sit on the floor, so that we could straddle his long legs. He allowed us to do that with great good humour, talking to us as equal to equal and making us talk. He always said that he learned as much from children as they learned from him.

6

For more than half a year, from February to October 1917, Russia was governed by a provisional government. This was a liberal government, which introduced freedom of speech and assembly and many other progressive measures. As seen by the Mensheviks, the February Revolution was a bourgeois revolution which, as good Marxists, they accepted as a necessary stage in history. They were accordingly happy to support the government in its reforms, while devoting their energies to the consolidation and furtherance of the rights of the industrial working class. Moreover, like the rest of the country, Mensheviks set their hopes on the Constituent Assembly, which was supposed to be held in the near future and which was expected to give the country a solid constitutional and legal structure. But meanwhile the war continued, and with it appalling hardships throughout the country – and this gave Lenin his chance.

Ever since he had returned to Russia in April, Lenin had devoted himself to strengthening Bolshevik influence in the soviets and the trade unions. He also commissioned Trotsky to train combat units, consisting mainly of sailors, for armed insurrection. With their help he arrested the members of the Provisional Government on 25 October (Old Style; by the Western calendar, the October Revolution took place on 7 November). He claimed to be taking power on behalf of the soviets; in reality he seized it on behalf of the Bolshevik Party, which until then had played a very minor part in the ongoing Revolution. To consolidate Bolshevik power he at once appointed Felix Dzerzhinsky to organise a new secret police, the Cheka.

The new Bolshevik government and all government offices soon moved to Moscow; and in their wake the central committees of all the major political parties did likewise. So early in 1918 Mother and I left Petrograd. It was a cold and windy morning when we made our way to the railway station for Moscow, the Nikolaevsky Vokzal. Inside the vast unlit station, every inch of space was covered with humanity. People were sitting or lying on the floors of the huge hall and the platforms beyond. We were told that there had been no train for days. It took us ages to get through the crowd and to find a small island on the platform where we could put down our two bundles and sit on them. Underfoot it was muddy and full of litter. No waiting-room or buffets were functioning. Only a few hot-water taps were in working order, and a long queue could be seen at each of these. But most people huddled motionless in the semi-darkness and semi-silence, listening for the train that did not come.

A little wizened old woman who had been sitting on her

bundle near us scrambled up and began to make her difficult way to the nearest hot-water tap, clutching her kettle. As I watched her slow progress through the crowd I saw her stumble and lose her grip on the kettle, the bright little copper pot rolled away from her and down to the rails. There was a great cry, half-moan and half-shriek, from the crowd, and then, from the opposite platform, a man jumped on to the rails and picked the kettle up. At this precise moment the long-awaited sound could be heard and the engine slowly chug-chugged its way into the station. There were shouts from all sides and arms stretched down to help the man up, but then our view was obscured by steam and smoke. Mother and I had recognised the man, it was a close friend of our family and one of the leaders of the Menshevik Party, Raphail Reine-Abramovich. Then the crowd surged forward, as if a great wind had risen and we were lifted up and swept along. We were irresistibly pulled and sucked into the train, where every inch of space seemed filled with people, on seats and between seats and in the corridors. People trod on our feet and we trod on theirs, but finally we edged our two bundles into a corner and sat on them. It was at least an hour before the train moved, but half-way through our wait, a young man could be seen fighting his way towards us, and though he never reached us, he managed to shout above the heads of the people: 'Raphail is safe . . . He was pulled out just in time!' We both felt like crying.

After what seemed like a lifetime we finally arrived in Moscow, cold, stiff and hungry. The city was crowded; not only Petrograd but the entire country seemed to have emptied itself into the new capital. On arrival we went straight to Mother's great friends, the Shers. The Shers were an old-established land-owning family. The widowed mother with several married sons and daughters and their children all lived in a roomy, old-fashioned house in an old-fashioned street, in an old-fashioned part of the town. The Ostozhenka was one of those narrow, winding Moscow streets where the houses were all of timber and the wide, gabled wooden gates led into inner yards with stables and outhouses. Most of the sons and daughters were active in the revolutionary movement, and the matriarch sympathised with that. Mother was a great favourite with the old lady and we were invited to stay as long as we wished.

I stood in awe of the old lady but took immediately to the old nurse Ignatievna, who had nursed two generations of Shers and still wielded power over the youngest. A small, compact old woman, rather like my own, dear Grandmother Sara, she was stern in manner but very patient with us children. After one day in her care I was totally devoted to her. Ignatievna was very pious and was deeply worried about the fate of her former nurselings, many of whom had been in prison. In 1905, the eldest son, Vasily, an army officer, had led his troops out in support of the Revolution. He had been sentenced to death for that and though he was reprieved, Ignatievna never recovered. She said that he and his brothers had 'sold their souls to the Antichrist', but still loved them and still prayed for them.

While the churches were still open – they were to be closed by government order later that year – Ignatievna often went to church and sometimes took some of the children with her. It was a late spring that year and at Easter there was still snow in the streets when Ignatievna took me and two other little girls, all of the same age, to an all-night Easter service in the lovely old church in the Ostozhenka. The little white church, almost round in shape and topped by golden domes, was barely visible under the dusky grey sky and against the white-grey snow on the ground. Inside, like all Russian churches, it was uncluttered by pews and chairs and had no windows at the ground level, so that the floor looked like a huge, dark saucer brimful with people. The dense crowd stood shoulder to shoulder, everyone facing the altar, and all enveloped in grey clouds of incense. The crowd seemed one single body; and it was warm from its breath.

Around the altar the many glimmering icons, the clusters of tall, lighted candles and the gold embroidered vestments of the clergy made an oasis of dazzling light. The clergy moved before us in a ritual ceremony, swinging censers and intoning prayers. Somewhere above our heads, from a gallery, an invisible choir responded. Sometimes we all knelt on the cold floor, and there was much scraping and shuffling as old women laboriously rose again, holding on to their neighbours and dragging their shoes over the flagstones. But most of the time the crowd was still, while the deep voice of the *dyakon* and the high responses of the choir soared to the vaults of the roof, taking, it seemed to me, our prayers and our souls up to the heavens. The night was long but nobody felt fatigue. We were all sustained by our closeness, secure, all of us, in the dark womb of the church. When dawn broke, the windows high above us grew lighter and all eyes turned towards them, while we ourselves were still in darkness. And the choir sang out, rejoicing.

After the service, the people filed out slowly, each one buying a candle and lighting it at the door. 'It's lucky,' said

Ignatievna, 'to bring the candle home still lit, to put it under your icon.' So we walked ever so slowly and ever so carefully, step by small step, shielding the feeble flame with the free hand. And all over the large open space around the church and along the streets leading away from it, stooping little figures could be seen in the uncertain light of a murky early morning, carrying their flickering candles home.

A few hours later, in the huge kitchen of the Sher house, the matriarch presided over the traditional Easter morning ceremony: all members of the family and all guests and all *chada* (servants and dependents) kissed her, and were kissed by her, on both cheeks, as she said: '*Khristos voskrese*' (Christ is risen) and they responded: '*Vo istinu voskrese*' ('In truth he is risen'). On the enormous kitchen table, covered with a white damask cloth, there were coloured eggs and all the other Easter dishes, though of course there was not the plenty of pre-war years.

All this gave me an unforgettable glimpse of Old Russia, a world which was about to disappear for ever.

In the summer of 1918, my brother Danya and I stayed a few weeks at one of the Shers' country estates. But this was no longer Old Russia, rather a Russia caught between the old and the new. The matriarch owned two estates in the Moscow region, but had, long before the Revolution, made one of them over to her two sons and two daughters, and they, in turn, had at once given most of the land away to the local peasants, keeping only the house and yard for themselves. The four new owners, all married and with children, shared the house for holidays, and they all worked together on the small home farm, where there were a few cows, two horses and some poultry. Of the numerous host of servants of former times, only two old men still lived on the estate, not so much to work as to teach their 'masters' how to farm.

Along with all the other children, Danya and I were allotted our duties around the house and given some animals to look after. My special task was to groom and feed a young mole-grey bull – 'a baby still', I was told, but quite strong enough to knock me off my feet when he felt playful. I doted on him. Danya helped the older boys with the care of the horses. Every morning they had to take the horses down to the stream, and as Danya did not know how to ride, the boys decided he should learn. So one morning, without waiting for instruction and without a saddle, he swung himself on to the back of one of the horses. It had always seemed a gentle animal, but it was so startled by this unusual behaviour that it bolted. In no time at all, horse and rider had disappeared into the far distance. We imagined all sorts of disasters. It was a bit of an anti-climax, or a relief, and a great triumph for the hero, when horse and rider reappeared hours later, Danya still clinging to the mane of the tired steed.

I learned less perilous skills. Every morning I drove the light one-horse open carriage to the post office in the nearest village to collect mail and newspapers. Old Yegor sat next to me, ready to seize the reins when danger loomed, which it invariably did when, on our return journey, we had to turn rather sharply from the narrow bridge on to our road. The playful young chestnut always tried to overturn the carriage at that spot if not prevented by old Yegor.

When the mushrooms began to appear, the whole household and several children from the village went on regular mushrooming forays. Each with a basket or a pot or a saucepan, we set out early to walk the few miles to the nearest mushroom forest. One of these expeditions I remember particularly well. It was a misty morning and the forest, when we reached it, seemed still to be holding a bit of the night. According to custom we dispersed over a large area, each being left on his or her own when collecting, so that there should be no trespassing on each other's territory. We all knew about mushrooms: which were the best, the firmest, which were good for pickling but not for frying, and, of course, which were poisonous. And we were not meant to stray beyond reach of the regular calls – 'Auuu, a-uu', which was the traditional mushrooming call. I was half-fearful, half-pleased to be left on my own, treated as it were as a grown-up. Bravely I made my way towards the tall oaks which, I knew, were the home of one of the bolitus mushrooms. To reach them I had to cross a pretty clearing with small bushes and tree-stumps and then get over a shallow ditch. It was when I jumped down the ditch that I saw a little animal. It was a wolf cub, a woolly, cuddly little cub and it was, if anything, more frightened than I was. What was I to do? I dared not call out to the others, lest the cub's mother come and 'eat' me; and I was too much of a coward to go on. I retreated stealthily until I was out of the ditch and then ran for my life. I was shaking with fright – but what a story to tell the others!

Those weeks on the Sher estate gave me a taste of care-free childhood such as I had not known since Minusinsk. It was to be my last.

Back in Moscow I found myself with Mother and, once again, alone with Mother. Father had remained in Petrograd, and all other members of the family had been sent by Mother away from hungry Moscow to places where there was more food. Danya went to Father's sister Fanny in faraway Tomsk, beyond the Urals. We were not to see him again for many years. Grandmother, our dear Babushka Sara, was dispatched to friends in Tambov, where she went missing. She was never heard of again, dying God knows when and God knows how. This was a time when all over Russia families were being torn apart by the Civil War.

Mother had great difficulty in finding lodgings for us in Moscow, but Father's youngest sister came to the rescue. Anna (or Khanochka as she was known in the family) was studying at Moscow University and lived in a small furnished room in the centre of the city. She offered to share it with us. It was at the table where she set out her meagre rations for us to share that I heard Mother speak about the general situation in the country. This was in a sense the beginning of my adult life. I was now nearly eleven and capable of following talk about politics. It was as if a curtain had been pulled aside. I could not understand everything that was said, but I got a general impression. I gathered that the Constituent Assembly, from which so much had been expected, had been dispersed by brute force as soon as it became clear that the electorate had voted overwhelmingly, not for the Bolsheviks but for the Social Revolutionaries. Everywhere non-Bolshevik socialists were being arrested and imprisoned. The offices of the Menshevik Party were raided, all documents removed and confiscated. Workers were rebelling against the Bolsheviks and they, too, were being arrested and imprisoned. Mother could scarcely believe what was happening: who would have imagined that revolutionaries would find themselves once again in prison, put there by a revolutionary party, by their former comrades? She felt that the Revolution, that radiant future to which she had devoted her life, was being ruined. She was deeply depressed.

As Mother saw it, the murder of the Tsar and his family, the execution of thousands of priests, the bloody oppression of the middle class and of the peasantry – all carried out on the orders of Lenin – had plunged the country into total chaos. The Mensheviks had protested against every one of these excesses – Martov in particular had published passionate denunciations of Bolshevik terror – but all protests had been ignored. There was worse to come. Civil War engulfed the country, from the shores of the Pacific to the Baltic and from Archangel to the Crimea. There were Red armies and White armies, and armed bands which called themselves Green and Black. Appalling atrocities were committed on all sides. The land was devastated.

7

LIFE IN MOSCOW was very difficult. Food was severely rationed, and even with ration cards was hard to find. And I still presented a problem, it seemed. Mother was kept very busy at the Menshevik Central Committee; she was out all and every day and most nights. Khanochka went every morning to her lectures and often worked late at the library. So what was to be done with me? School was out of the question, since very few schools were open. But, said Khanochka, why not give me into the care of her fiancé Lyova Mirsky, who was in charge of a military hospital train stationed at one of Moscow's railway stations, and who actually lived in the train? He was a busy man, but he would keep me out of trouble and share his lunch with me.

It seemed an excellent idea to them; to me it spelled being again relegated to the nursery. Still, it promised much more

freedom and even some adventure and was certainly prefer-
able to being dumped on yet another family. And so I was
taken every morning by either Mother or Khanochka to a
large railway terminus, through a vast booking hall, along the
whole length of the platforms and over a labyrinth of rails
to where the hospital train stood. It struck me at once that
the steps to the train started higher above the ground than
was usual when a train stood at a platform. I had to swing
myself up by the arms to reach the lowest step. This was
great fun and getting on and off the steps became my main
occupation during the days that followed – childish perhaps
but it kept me happy. I must have climbed them hundreds of
times – 'a thousand at least', said Lyova (or Lyovushka, as we
called him). He was a jovial, kindly young man with a closely
shaved round head and a broad grin on his pink face that
made him look like the sun in children's books. He was a
great athlete, and later he was to become one of the founders of Maccabi, the Jewish sports club and, later still, a professor at the Institute for Physical Culture in Moscow. We got
along splendidly. I was not allowed to stray from the train or
to loiter inside it, but I was not bored; I felt this to be my train
and wove unending dream stories about my travels in it. As
usual I was really happiest when left to myself.

At midday Lyovushka called me into his compartment,
half-office, half-bedroom, and we had a meal together. Since
he received army rations, these lunches seemed feasts to me.
And after lunch I was tucked in on Lyovushka's cot, which I
considered the height of luxury, and I either slept or read
until Lyovushka returned from duty in the wards, further
down the train. Mother or Khanochka were often quite late
collecting me, so I had plenty of time to read.

While we were staying with Khanochka we regularly went to the public baths. In the street, a change of clothes and a piece of soap wrapped in a towel and a large shawl wrapped around head and shoulders denoted prospective bathers, and the nearer one got to the familiar large building with two wings – Men and Women – the more numerous such figures became. Russians love public baths and there was an air of festivity about the whole thing. One entered a large ante-room with cubicles, one stripped, took a large wooden scoop with a handle for scooping up hot and cold water, finally one went into the main room, and was at once surrounded by naked women of all ages and every shape. Public baths are great levellers. Those who had never had a private bathroom and those, like us, who temporarily did not have the use of one, were all equal and all happily splashed ourselves with hot water or rested on the long wooden benches in the warm steam.

Young women with round stomachs and with flat stomachs, broad hips and narrow hips, small breasts and large breasts, some with bobbed hair and some with hair hanging to their buttocks; and old women with shrivelled arms, stomachs, breasts – it was a complete panorama of female humanity. I got so used to seeing all this that for the rest of my life nudity has remained for me as natural as earth and sky. I was particularly drawn to old women. Looking from their wrinkled faces to their shrivelled bodies I thought of Babushka Sara and felt love and tenderness for them all.

That same year, in Moscow, I was taken to the opera for the first time in my life. It was a splendid performance of Rimsky-Korsakov's *Sadko*. The spectacle on the stage completely absorbed my attention, so that I hardly heard the music. The big ship, all painted rigging and sails, actually heaved on to the stage, blue waves billowing around it. The sailors climbed up and down and looked very busy and sang, sang, sang. And then – heavens – the ship wobbled and toppled and the tall mast keeled right over into the stalls! There were screams in the audience, and on the stage people could be seen scrambling out from underneath the huge blue canvas, leaving the 'waves' flat and flabby. Luckily nobody was hurt, the mast having come to rest just above the heads of the spectators. But it was frightening and, naturally, for me, it was the high point of the opera.

Towards the end of 1918 we returned to Petrograd. But we did not find Father there; he had been called to Vilna, where his mother was very ill. She died a few hours after his arrival. He was told that she had stayed alive by sheer willpower, asking all the time whether her beloved Motik had arrived and determined to see him once more before she died. Father's father had died some time earlier, of starvation it was said, as he had no money to buy food. Yet after his death they found the drawers of his desk stuffed with bank-notes. He had been a highly respected lawyer in Vilna and one of the three members of the Jewish arbitration court, to which local Jews brought their complaints and conflicts, as they did not trust the Russian courts. The party found guilty by the arbitrators had to promise to set the wrong right and as a token of good faith deposited a certain sum of money. This was kept in trust by one of the arbitrators and returned to the depositor when he had expiated his wrongdoing. If he failed to do so, the money was paid to the wronged party. It was these deposits which were found in the old lawyer's desk. He had died rather than touch them.

After his mother's death, Father made several attempts to return to Petrograd, but the Civil War was so intense that he was twice caught and almost shot as a spy. In the end he gave up his attempts and went to Warsaw and then to Vienna, where his only brother was living.

Mother and I, meanwhile, were facing the same problems as in Moscow: finding a place to live, getting food and so on. Things were different in Petrograd: food was even scarcer, public transport and public services had become non-existent, and instead of overcrowding there were many empty, half-derelict houses in which nobody lived. But we were lucky: soon after our arrival, Mother was stopped in the street by a man whom she had known before the Revolution. He was a banker, a rich man, but he had sympathised with liberals and even with revolutionaries and had occasionally helped them financially. Now, of course, as a bourgeois, he went in fear of his life and had thought it wise to change his address. He offered Mother the use of his luxurious apartment in the previously fashionable Furshtatskaya Street, next to the former American Embassy. His motives were not entirely unselfish: an apartment that stood empty was in danger of requisition. Mother had no illusions, 'unpaid caretaker', she said; but she was glad to accept.

The apartment turned out to be very large and contained two 'unpaid caretakers', two elderly spinster sisters, distant relatives of the banker's wife. They were timid and kindly and easy to get on with. We shared the kitchen with them; and of the innumerable bedrooms, they occupied one and Mother and I another; the bathroom was unusable as all the taps and

pipes were broken and there was no hot water. In the middle
of the flat, a vast and beautifully furnished drawing-room was
taken over by rats, which nested in the upholstered settees
and in the grand piano. On the way to our bedrooms we had
to cross that room each night and I clung to Mother's skirts
in terror. It was in the kitchen that we mainly lived, as it was
the only room that could be heated, on and off, by a cast-iron
studio stove, the so-called *burzhuyka* (bourgeoise). This had to
be fed with logs or coke, which were rationed. We shared our
fuel rations and often our food rations as well, as it took less
fuel to cook for four than for two separate families.

In the evenings the two sisters retired early to bed, taking
a pot of hot water with them, to wash in their bedroom.
Mother and I washed ourselves in the kitchen, huddling over
the stove. Part of the nightly ritual was the combing of my
hair for lice. Even more than rats, lice seemed to thrive that
year in Petrograd; they were, of course, carriers of disease,
and huge posters all over town urged us to 'take part in the
campaign of lice extermination'. So I submitted patiently to
the slow, careful combing with the fine comb, while we talked
over the events of the day and made plans for tomorrow. It
was the most intimate, cosiest moment of our day.

There were several apartments like ours in the house, originally the homes of rich people, but now occupied, the sisters
said, by people 'who do not belong here'. There was a house
committee, which distributed fuel, when available, and allocated duties, such as sweeping the stairs, the courtyard and
the street outside the gates. In winter the duties included
clearing the snow and, as the Civil War had moved nearer,
guarding the gates day and night, with loaded rifles. The
house committee was the last link in the chain of officialdom

that regulated our lives; not yet quite the bureaucracy of later years, but a portent of it. Our lives were lived under the all-seeing, all-registering eye of the house committee. Without the signature of its chairman or secretary, we did not exist; they had to testify that we were residing at such and such an address and that we were legitimate recipients of ration cards or of any of the innumerable permits and passes, without which we could get nothing and go nowhere.

In the early days of our life in the Furshtatskaya, my main duty was to queue for food. Mother had to leave home early to go to work – I never knew where she worked but rather assumed that it was in the Menshevik Party offices – and I walked with her as far as the food distribution store. However early I arrived, there was always a long queue already in place, but not moving. Shops on both sides of the store were boarded up, as indeed were all shops, even along the Liteyny, but there was always a crowd before the food store. The door of the store was firmly closed and there was no telling when it would open. Quite often it was midday before it did, either to admit the queue or, simply, to allow a large dirty placard to be inserted into the door-frame saying: 'No distribution of food today' or 'Bread and salt only today', or 'Bread and *vobla* (dried salt fish)' or '*Vobla* only today'. In theory we were supposed to receive bread, fats, sugar and meat, but supplies of all these goods were in desperately short supply.

Mother had told me not to sit on the cold kerbstones but I usually did, and sometimes I even dozed off, tightly clutching our ration cards in both hands. These long waits were irredeemably grey – the dusty, boarded-up fronts of shops, the shabbily dressed people, the murky light, the drizzle. And the mood of the queue was grey too, though sometimes it could turn ugly, when somebody jumped the queue or the supplies failed to arrive. I was glad then to be small and would make myself even smaller, though when it came to brawls, children got their share of cuffs.

Most people were able to supplement their rations with some kind of midday snack, usually a bowl of soup or gruel, at their place of work. Most 'enterprises' (in officialese everything was called that, from factories to theatres) were supplied with these small meals. I don't suppose that the Menshevik Party offices qualified as an 'enterprise' and Mother certainly did not get any snacks there. But, luckily, she had an entrée to the Dom Poetov (House of Poets), a club of writers, painters and actors and the like, which was a recognised 'enterprise'. Mother had always been a translator (from the English), and recently her translations of Jack London had taken the first prize in a competition organised by the State Publishing House for Foreign Literature. Good translators have always enjoyed great prestige in Russia, so this success entitled Mother to membership of the House of Poets. As family members were also admitted, I went there every day. I loved it. It made me feel great to sit at or near the tables where Alexander Blok and Anna Akhmatova and other great poets held court. Much noisier were the tables of the painters and actors, who seemed all to be talking at the same time, gesticulating and laughing. Being a small and shy girl I did not intrude, but the painters and actors were very friendly, waving to me, taking me on their knees, getting me to laugh at their jokes.

There was a bar along one side of the room, and though it was quite bare – most days there was no food or cigarettes – one could usually get a cup of hot tea, or at least of hot water. That warmed one a bit. And once, in the spring of 1919 (or was it 1920?) there was a sensation: glasses of sour milk were doled out at the bar, one glass per person. Though the Russian word for sour milk, *prostokvasha*, evokes nothing so much as a wet rag, that event inspired several cabaret songs – not perhaps profound but full of feeling:

'Ah, *prostokvasha*, you are our joy,

Ah, *prostokovasha, prostokvasha, prostokvasha. . .*'

But such treats were rare.

8

Meanwhile mother had decided that I could remain ignorant and untutored no longer; I must go to school. This met with passionate opposition from me. I was not ignorant; since we moved into the flat in the Furshtatskaya, I had discovered the shelves full of books in one of the rooms. There was nobody to direct my reading, so I devoured indiscriminately Russian classics and foreign classics in Russian translation. From Dickens's fog-bound Thames and London docks, to Victor Hugo's slums of Paris and Jack London's Arctic wastes, there was no land I had not lived in in my imagination. And nearer home – Dostoevsky's grey and gloomy St Petersburg, Gogol's colourful Ukrainian villages and Chekhov's and Zamyatin's sweet-sour short stories – all were familiar to me. I was, in fact, a widely read eleven-year-old. And poets! When I was not writing poetry myself (a fact

I did not mention to Mother), I was reading it. Lermontov was my hero, and, of the moderns, Alexander Blok and Nikolay Gumilev. I could think of nothing more wonderful than to have my nose in a book, even when the *burzhuyka* had gone out and I had to wrap myself in a blanket. Besides, I had always been alone and school scared me out of my wits – but that, too, I did not tell Mother.

And Mother was adamant. There was, she said, quite near our house, on the famous old street, the Ligovka, a school founded before the Revolution by a family of well-known liberal educationalists: that would do nicely. It was a boys' school, but this did not worry Mother; a government decree issued some months earlier had made all schools co-educational. True, people seemed slow to send their daughters to boys' schools, and the one on the Ligovka numbered as yet no girls among its pupils. But this did not worry Mother either; there must always be a first to seize any opportunity offered, so I was taken to the headmaster, inscribed into the junior school and told to report next day. This was the beginning of six months of martyrdom. The boys were outraged at the intrusion of a mere girl and determined to get rid of the intruder by making life hell for her. In class, my thick plaits of hair were nailed to the desk behind me, ink was spilled over my clothes and books, I was pinched and cuffed whenever the teacher's back was turned. Worst of all was the cold dislike and contempt shown me by the boys, from the youngest to the oldest (boys of senior school next door were forever coming over to join in the persecution). All of them believed that if they succeeded in driving me out, no more girls would come.

I could not fight back – how could I, alone against so many? But I got so angry (my hair *was* red!) that I was determined not to give in, not to beg for mercy. So I didn't complain to Mother or the teachers and if I cried, I cried in secret. As it turned out, I had my reward. Some few months later the authorities enforced compulsory co-education, by putting half of each class of the boys' schools into the corresponding classes of girls' schools in the same area and vice versa. Our school was suddenly flooded with girls and it was obviously no good trying to oust them all. Overnight my position changed: I was no longer a 'repulsive toad', a 'carrot-headed monster'; suddenly I was everybody's darling, 'one of us', an 'old timer'. It was hugely gratifying.

During breaks I could mingle and chat with the boys, while the 'new' girls walked somewhat sullenly up and down the big hall speaking only to one another. Sometimes, before or after school, I went with some of the boys to the small open-air market across the street. It was fun walking between the stalls and looking at the wares, though I cannot remember anything but old clothes being offered; and on two stalls, coloured strips of paper and pencils, highly valued by the boys. But the great attraction for me was the old, toothless Chinese man who could be found some mornings sitting on the kerb outside the market, playing his one-string violin. This he scratched on a piercingly high note as he sang, in a piercingly high voice, a Chinese song. It sounded to me like so many 'aaas' and 'ooos' – monotonous and ear-splitting, almost painful to listen to, but quite hypnotic. As were the old man's crab-apple face of a hundred wrinkles and the grin of his toothless mouth. Somehow I linked him in my memory to the old Kirghizes whom I had seen in the market of Minusinsk, and my heart warmed to him.

One day Grisha, the most popular senior boy, came over

to our side of the school and sought me out specially. He was the scoutmaster of the Boy Scouts' troop at the school and he had orders 'from above' to organise a girls' troop; would I join it and help him to recruit other girls? I was very flattered and, of course, agreed at once. Soon there were quite a few girls joining, and an older girl, Marusya, was appointed leader of the Girl Guides; she at once appointed me her adjutant. And then both Boy Scouts and Girl Guides were amalgamated into a single troop and renamed Red Scouts. We were given smart khaki uniforms: pleated skirts for girls and shorts for boys, but for the rest identical long, belted tunics, yellow kerchiefs, knee-socks and a beautiful whistle on a long cord. I still have a rather blurred photo (the only one of all those years) of me in my uniform. I doubt that Mother was particularly pleased with all this but I was so obviously happy with my new friends that she tolerated even the mock military uniform. Besides, it saved such a lot of clothes' coupons!

During the long break we drilled in the long hall. Or, sitting on the floor cross-legged in groups of ten or twelve, we practised map-reading and learned various skills. And Grisha lectured on the traditional tasks and duties of Scouts and we all glowed with zeal to be 'always ready' to help the helpless, to succour the infirm and to make ourselves generally useful. We could not foresee how soon we would indeed have to make ourselves useful, and on a much greater scale and in many more ways than we had been taught by Grisha.

Grisha also told us about the origins of the Scout movement. It was thrilling to learn that it all started in England, that faraway glorious country of Dickens and Byron and Darwin. It was wonderful to think that we were learning and doing the same things as our English brothers and sisters. And we even went camping, I remember, assembling at a small railway station somewhere beyond the Smolny Institute, and boarding a suburban train for the country. To 'toughen' us Grisha gave orders that we should jump off the train *before* we reached a certain station. I clearly remember the cold terror that paralysed me as I was standing on the lowest step below the carriage door – less fear of jumping than fear of being too cowardly to jump. In the event, the boys behind me simply pushed me off. I rolled down a steep grassy slope and landed in a thicket of brambles and nettles. I was not the only one: howls of pain could be heard all along the line. We were then made to march through the forest to the clearing where we were to camp. The misery of stings, cuts and bruises spoilt the day for me and I remember nothing about erecting tents and lighting the camp fire by rubbing two sticks together, all of which had been the reason for our going to the country. Fortunately we never again went camping in my time.

Marusya often took me about with her – I suspected to make herself important. 'This is my adjutant,' she used to say. Most often we went to the Smolny Institute, a former boarding school for daughters of the nobility and particularly those destined for service at the Imperial Court. In 1917 the school was closed and after Lenin's coup the building housed the headquarters of the Bolshevik Party. We went there to visit Marusya's particular friends, the daughters of the former cook to the Institute. She was now cooking for the canteen of the Bolsheviks and continued to live, with her family, in their former quarters. On our arrival we usually got a tasty bite of something or other and then the cook's younger daughters and I went out into the gardens, leaving the others to their gossip in the wide, gleaming kitchen. The gardens were really a large park, where the former pupils, the *institutki*, used to walk demurely along the gravelled paths. The paths were no longer very tidy and there were many places where the bushes had grown into wildernesses. It was there that we loved to play hide and seek. But when we were spotted, we were warned off by the sentries patrolling the park.

Once there was a real alarm: Trotsky happened to be staying at the Smolny and it was rumoured that there was to be an attempt on his life. A swarm of soldiers was sent into the gardens to search every nook. We did not wait for them; my playmates took me down a dark passage at the back of the grounds into the adjoining Smolny Cathedral. This passage had been used by the *institutki* in their time, but now the door was overgrown with moss and very hard to open. Inside the passage smelt damp and mouldy. We pulled the door behind us and then gently tiptoed in the darkness, until we came to a heavy curtain. We pulled this aside and suddenly we stood under the immense dome, in the vast emptiness of the cathedral. It was the most beautiful place I had ever seen, and the most mysterious. Even neglected and dusty as they had become since the Revolution, the icons on the walls gleamed. The faint light from the windows high above picked out the dark faces on the icons and the tarnished gold of their frames, and played on the many railings and screens. In its desolation the place was still awe-inspiring. But this was no living church, it was the realm of the dead.

We stayed hours inside the cathedral, afraid of going back into the gardens the way we had come, until the chill and the fading light drove us out at last. We made for the main gates of the Smolny. The sentries knew my two companions but would not let me in without a pass. They were bad-tempered: the supposed would-be assassin had not been found and the sentries had been blamed for his escape. At length the cook was summoned to vouch for me and I was allowed to enter. But that day passes were checked and rechecked, so Marusya and I were late in leaving and I was late back home. I was careful not to offer Mother any explanation: what would she say to my dodging armed soldiers in the Smolny grounds!

Sometimes Marusya took me to a scoutmaster called Alexey. He had a room in an apartment house near the intersection of the Nevsky and the Liteyny Prospekts – which formerly would have been a most fashionable address. It was a marvellous room: floors, walls, doors and even the wide couch were covered with Persian rugs and carpets, and there were swords, daggers and pistols everywhere. I believe Alexey must have inherited the room from his elder brother who had been an officer in the Tsar's army. But Alexey led us to believe that all this décor, and particularly the weapons, were his. Certainly he knew how to use them. His favourite pastime was pistol practice: he would place Marusya or me in a chair against the wall and then shoot all around us, just as they do it at the fairs. We were petrified but, of course, we were honour bound not to show panic. His neighbours did not mind or perhaps were too petrified to complain.

At times Alexey was brooding and a little sinister; at others he would be loving to me, while barely polite to Marusya, who was only too obviously in love with him. I could see that there was some kind of game being played between them and that Marusya was no match for him. Sometimes, to spite her, he invited me alone and I did not know whether I should go. But Marusya crossly said that of course I must go, because he was higher in rank. I was perplexed to know what it had to do with rank, but I really loved to go. With me he was always relaxed and friendly and gave me sweets. He still liked to practise with the pistols but seemed more careful, and I trusted him. Still, on the whole I was relieved when he left the city and so, I suspect, was Marusya.

Spring 1919: the Civil War, which was in full swing elsewhere, had not yet reached Petrograd. But already the city bore a drained, hushed look. Government offices and all other public bodies had moved to Moscow, most of the menfolk were away at the various fronts, and the food situation and public transport were deteriorating steadily. People in the streets looked tired and dispirited.

And yet life went on somehow, including cultural life, which went on feverishly. We went to hear Chaliapin in Glinka's *Russlan and Ludmilla* in the Mariinsky Opera House. To get there we trudged for what seemed hours through the streets empty of any kind of traffic. But the Mariinsky seemed as festive as ever. Chaliapin sang the part of the fat knight, a part with little singing really but he acted superbly. When this cowardly knight found himself alone in a darkening wood, having lost his way and his mount, he seemed to shrink with fright, screwing his legs around each other like corkscrews and stumbling round the stage like a drunk. His head, which looked like a ball, sank into a short neck and his body, too, looked round; only the legs were spindly. In later years I saw him act thin men with long necks and narrow heads, such as Don Quixote, equally convincingly. We also went to concerts. The pianist Zillotti was then very popular and we went to hear him play Beethoven. The hall was usually unheated and the old man had to rub his hands and blow on his fingers before he could play. It was my first taste of classical music and for a long time afterwards I dreamed of becoming a pianist. To the present day, the piano is my favourite instrument.

On the ninth anniversary of Tolstoy's death, Maxim Gorky was to speak in one of the largest halls in Petrograd. Long before the appointed time the hall is packed; those who have no seats stand along the walls in a dense crowd or climb up on to the window sills. The platform is very large and as Gorky slowly comes forward to the lectern, one can see that he is a very sick man. When he begins to speak, his voice is so feeble that it can hardly be heard at the back of the hall. The audience holds its breath; not a sound, not a cough interrupts Gorky's communion with the dead Tolstoy. Slowly he proceeds down the path of the years, remembers his visits to the Great Master, repeats his very words. And then, in the middle of a sentence his breath fails him: 'when the cable came . . . Lev Nikolaevich . . . I would not . . . could not believe it!' Helplessly, blindly he gropes for the water jug and his head, the grey, stubbly head of a walrus, flops down on his arms and his shoulders shake. Gorky weeps, weeps wordlessly – Tolstoy is dead . . . For a moment, the audience is stunned; most of us have not yet grasped what he said. But a murmur passes from row to row till it reaches the back wall. And just as Gorky lifts his head again, trying to speak, the wave of emotion flows back to him – sobs around here and there, gathering in strength. And Gorky has to stop, breaks down anew. The tide flows to and from him; each new hesitation, each break in his voice is answered by renewed sobbing. He can do no more, he turns and stumbles from the platform. Now indeed the dam breaks: the crowd surrenders itself to tears. What are we crying about – the dead Tolstoy, the half-dead Gorky? Who knows? We are all half-dead, worn out, and it takes little to make us cry.

That spring I walked a lot through the streets, all by myself. This was the time of my final discovery of St Petersburg – Petrograd – 'Pieter'. And discovering it meant falling in love with it. As I walked I had an unending dialogue with the stones and with those large, heavy slabs of granite that covered the embankments, the roads, the pavements. They felt companionable and friendly under my feet. Not so the huge empty spaces of which there were so many in Pieter: the Senate Square, the Mars Field, the approaches to all the big palaces. These were intimidating and I had to brace myself before crossing them. There were hardly any cars in those days, only some army lorries on the main thorough-fares; and only a few trams were still in working order. For that matter there were very few pedestrians about in the middle of the morning. So I had it all to myself. And the wide River Neva drew me, so majestic and smooth on quiet days, so stormy on breezy days. When it was stormy I could hear Pushkin's Iron Rider, the statue of Peter the Great in the Senate Square, gallop through the roaring gale and the floods threatening the city; and sheer terror gripped me by the throat.

In June–July the White Nights took the city over – and White Night meant no night, the sun did not set and daylight did not wane. The city was bathed in a light half-moon, half-sun, translucent, yet mysterious. Even indoors I could not sleep and was tense, waiting for something. I don't know why but I was afraid of White Nights.

But on sunny mornings, to see the city so clearly, so beautifully on both sides of the Neva, the houses so well proportioned and graceful, the golden domes of the cathedrals and the spires of the Admiralty and of the Peter and Paul Fortress glittering so brightly in the sun – could anything be more wonderful? And away from the river, inland, there were the innumerable canals, crossed by graceful bridges with statues and lovely candelabra-like street lamps. I would stand forever on some bridge, looking towards the next bridge. In the streets flanking the canals were semi-basement shops, just like the grocery where I used to buy myself a slice of hot buttered bread – in, what seemed to me, a previous existence. No hot buttered bread to be had now! The only hope of appeasing my gnawing hunger was to get to the House of Poets and scrounge something to eat there.

After a long morning's wanderings I was glad too of the company. I could always be sure of an affectionate welcome at the actors' table, particularly from the actors of the Gaydeburov Theatre. Gaydeburov was the leading actor, director and producer of a co-operative repertory company, which shared all the profits and all the expenses, as well as all the work, in the cosy little theatre of its own. I had boundless admiration for Gaydeburov, but my special friend was the comic. He must have been fat once but in those hungry years nobody stayed fat, only the empty folds of skin around his neck and waist bore witness to his former shape. But his face was still round and his eyes were two twinkly slits. I loved him very much, my very own pal.

The Gaydeburov Theatre specialised in Scandinavian plays; Gaydeburov himself was at his brilliant best in plays by Ibsen, Strindberg, Björnson. Despite lack of transport the theatre was always full: Petrograders were prepared to walk miles for a concert, a poetry reading or a play, and in fact all theatres were full to overflowing. The main difficulty was electricity – sometimes it would not come on at all, at other times it might be switched off in the middle of the performance. In such cases the audience and the actors in full costume and make-up would all flock on to the street and stand on the pavement, while somebody was dispatched to the nearest electricity office to find out about the prospects for the rest of the evening. That somebody was sometimes me – I had been accepted by the troupe as a messenger and general dogsbody and, dressed as I was, in my Red Scout uniform, I felt myself invested with semi-official status. When the lights were on and the performance took place, I always had a free seat in the stalls. At twelve I probably understood only vaguely what the plays were all about, but I felt passionately and intensely for all the characters. I remember one evening when Gaydeburov was acting a pastor in a play by Björnson – I forget the name of the play – and the pastor's soul, as I understand, was divided between his love for God and his love for a woman. There was a scene when the woman was dying and the pastor used all his spiritual power, all the power of prayer, to keep her alive. The tension was unbearable, until she slowly stirred and lifted first her head and then her body from the couch. Without knowing it I was also rising slowly, slowly in my seat – until a hand pressed me down from behind, shattering my trance.

9

In october 1919 the Civil War reached Petrograd. A White army under General Yudenich surrounded the city. Supply routes were cut and food became even scantier than before. Artillery and rifle fire could be heard quite clearly. Groups of men with spades over their shoulders were seen making for the suburbs to dig trenches. All available military units were already there. Soon the city was drained of adult men and women and even of older boys. Grisha, my scoutmaster, had been swept straight from school into the army and was now an officer. He and a small group of equally young men, many of pre-shaving age, were leaving for the front; I was waiting at the gate to wave to him. He looked quite splendid, I thought, astride a horse, but the smile with which he acknowledged my wave was rather uncertain.

Compared with the blockade of Leningrad by the Germans in the Second World War, our earlier siege was a small affair: there was no aerial bombardment and no long-range artillery bombardment. Still, we suffered hunger and cold, and many died of cholera or typhus. Though the defenders had little ammunition they were prepared to defend every bridge and every street of the city. By night all house doors and gates were locked and the residents stood guard outside. When it was our turn, Mother collected a rifle from the house committee and she and I sat down for our vigil on small stools outside our entrance. The unlit street was deserted save for the muffled-up 'sentries' in front of each house. Nobody spoke, we all listened to the distant gunfire; wasn't it coming nearer? Houses on the opposite side of the street seemed to me insubstantial in the dusk, no more solid than theatrical backcloth, and I wove endless stories about the people who lived in them, all mysterious and sinister.

Probably Yudenich's units were as poorly fed and poorly armed as ours, for the siege was eventually lifted without the city surrendering. But by then all cats, dogs and horses had been eaten. I don't remember that there was any improvement in our material situation after the siege ended; if anything it was getting worse, with the winter approaching. I suppose Moscow too had little enough food and fuel itself to spare anything for us. Our weekly rations dwindled to half a piece of fudge or *pastila* (small squares of pressed fruit paste) instead of sugar, and very small quantities of butter or meat. Bread, which was also rationed, was of such poor quality, mainly chaff, that many people developed throat inflammation from eating it. Milk was hardly ever available – gone

were the days of the cheerful Finnish peasant women bringing milk into Pieter on horse carts. Only the dreadful *vobla*
was to be had at all easily.

I remember one 'feast' during that time: we were celebrat-
ing my friend Igor's birthday. His mother, Tanya Valgeanich,
was a very close friend of my parents from their shared
Siberian exile in 1902–3. In the aftermath of the 1905
Revolution Tanya's husband perished on the gallows and the
young widow was left with a baby boy. One of their fellow
exiles, Peter Garvi, described Tanya and her husband as the
most touching and attractive young couple, and as long as I
had known her she had preserved an ethereal kind of beauty.
By now her face was almost transparent.

Tanya and Igor often came to see us and on the occasion
of his birthday the two mothers had managed to assemble
some extra supplies: a little grey-looking flour and a few
carrots. With the help of these treats they concocted a
birthday dinner of three courses! First came the soup of
carrots in hot water, then a pie made of flour mixed with
water and stuffed with chopped carrots, and 'tea' (plain hot
water) with half a fudge each. We sat over this meal for a
long time at the kitchen table, relishing every bite and sip,
and when we finished, Igor patted his tummy and said with
feeling: 'If only we could have such a feast every day!'
Afterwards, I remember, Igor, who was two years older
than I was, taught me to dance the Polish *krakowiak* and the
Hungarian national dance. We both wore overcoats and
valenki (thick felt boots) and woollen mittens, as the
burzhuyka was giving out little heat. Mother and Tanya
laughed as they saw us falling over each other – 'two
dancing bears!' said Tanya. But in the end we danced quite

well together. It was the party of the year; in fact, I do not remember another.

After the long summer vacation, teaching had hardly restarted at school for lack of teachers, paper and books, and with the approach of winter it stopped altogether. Ink was frozen in the inkwells of unheated classrooms. And in the recreation hall wind whistled through holes in the window. But the caretaker Semyonich opened the school doors every weekday morning and lit the small cast-iron stove in a corner of the entrance hall. So each day we all made our way to school, walking in the slush in the middle of the streets, as the sidewalks were too slippery: snow had not been cleared for months and had frozen hard after alternate thaws and frosts. Bad enough if the surfaces had been flat, but all around the water spouts there were veritable hillocks of sheer ice, translucent, solid ice. How could one resist climbing them? But of course one slipped and landed, with a terrific bang, on one's bottom.

How different school was from a year ago! No more Chinese fiddlers on the corners, the market deserted, empty of stalls and of people. Once inside the school, we all crowded into the corner round the stove. But warming up was not always bliss; as our feet began to thaw, there were howls of pain all around: since no shoes had been obtainable in the city for a long time, we all wore shoes one or two sizes too small. And most of us had frostbite as well. As the feet got warm, the skin seemed to burn and the pain was excruciating – we called it Chinese torture. Huddled around the stove, the smaller fry crying and the others howling, we were nevertheless prepared to endure it all, knowing that there was a treat coming: after an hour or two of waiting the mobile

My mother, Eva Broido,
as the archetypal young revolutionary
and in her best clothes.

The author, aged about three, before I went to Siberia.

My father with Sanya and Galya in Yakutsk, Siberia.

My mother and grandmother with my half-sister
Sanya, and baby brother Danya, in Yakutsk.

The Yakutsk prison group after the mutiny, with my two half-sisters Galya and Sanya.

Exiles in Minusinsk, Siberia.

My parents' revolutionary
friends:
(right) Yuli Martov and
(below) Lydia Dan.

Pavel Axelrod.

Vera Zasulich as a young woman.

Yuli Martov with Fyodor Dan.

A group of Mensheviks in Berlin around 1926.

My father (left) with Frederic Voigt.

(Above left) The author as a Red Scout in Petrograd in 1919.
(Above) My brother Danya in Berlin in 1923.
(Left) My mother shortly before her return to Russia.

Alexandra Exter in
Paris.

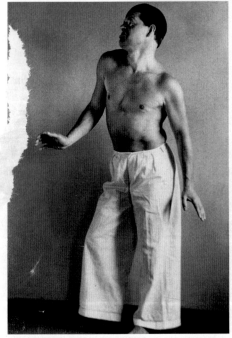

Raoul Hausmann as dancer.

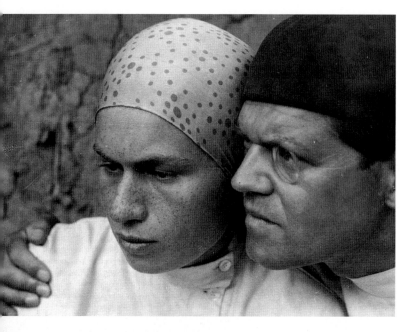

The author with Raoul Hausmann around 1929.

Ibiza in the early 1930s.

The author in England, 1937.

kitchen would arrive and each of us would get a bowl of hot gruel! When we had eaten and dispersed – a much happier crowd of children – Semyonich locked up the school.

Throughout 1919, the Red Scouts were called upon to perform all kinds of semi-official duties. During the siege, for instance, there were few ambulances for civilian use and few hospital porters or orderlies, so every morning our first job was to call at the hospital to which we were assigned and get a list of its requirements. I had been promoted and now had a sort of adjutant or assistant of my own – a small boy of seven or eight, a cub really. Usually we were given a sledge or a cart and, so equipped, we went briskly on our rounds: collecting and delivering medical supplies and food for 'our' hospital, taking messages to electricity or telephone offices or to other hospitals. At the worst period many people collapsed or died in the streets from either famine or disease, and we loaded them on to our sledge or cart and dragged them to the nearest hospital or emergency centre. When not so occupied we took up a position on some important corner, ready for a crisis. My little assistant tended to panic when left on his own, but he knew that a blast on his whistle would bring me running to his aid. We worked well as a team. And though probably very few citizens of that exhausted and starving city were even aware of us, we were very proud of our work.

Once, when I had carted a feeble old woman to hospital, she begged me not to leave her; she clung to me so fiercely that the nurse had difficulty in detaching her from me, and I had to promise her that I would come to see her next day. But on the morrow I found that she had been transferred to another hospital, right out in the harbour area. There were no trams going out to the harbour and I set off rather reluctantly on the long trudge. I had been told that the hospital was half-way along the road to the harbour, but not that it was a very long road.

To me that road seemed endless and more and more frightening: I had to pass derelict warehouses with gaping black gates and broken windows. Then suddenly, on the far side of the road, I saw a drunk lying half-in and half-out of a wide and dark cavern of a derelict and doorless house, and there were rats swarming all over him. The twitching body was pulled this way and that way like a rag doll and it was impossible to tell whether the man was dead or alive. I took to my heels, shaking with horror, and never stopped until I reached the hospital. And then I was sorry I came – the old woman turned out to be greedy and altogether hateful. She seized the bottle of milk I had brought for her and hid it from other patients; she never thanked me or asked whether I had milk for myself. In fact I had been lucky to get any milk at all and I had taken all of it to her, keeping it a secret even from Mother. I left her as soon as I could and then ran as fast as possible, without looking to left or right, my mind full of lurking horrors. I only stopped running when I was back in the centre of town, among other people.

10

I HAD GIVEN UP going for long walks, exploring new districts or revisiting familiar places that I loved. Walking was no longer a pleasure. My Pieter – always so trim and beautiful – was now drab and murky. Roads and pavements were covered with slush and filthy with litter; paint was peeling off the lovely façades on the embankment and many windows were broken or dirty or both. Pieter, like its inhabitants, had fallen on bad times.

1920: there was still little change in general but there was a change for the worse in our personal affairs. Mother was coughing at night, a painful, dry little cough which sometimes woke me up. When the doctor came to see her he said it was almost certainly to do with the lungs, only he could not be certain without proper tests and it would be difficult to get them done. Hospitals were not working as they should and medicines were not available. So he went away, shaking his head. Meanwhile Mother could hardly drag herself to work and grew thinner by the day. I had seen enough death in the streets to know how ill she was. In bed at night I wondered what would become of me if she died. Our immediate family was dispersed all over Russia and the nearest relative, a brother of Father's, was in Vienna. If only she could get me there, but how could she, ill and penniless as she was?

Then, coming home one day I found her packing; we were going away, abroad, but nobody must know about it. The most amazing piece of luck: she had met in the street her old acquaintance, the banker, in whose flat we were living, and he had offered to include us in a small group of people with whom he himself planned to cross the border into Poland. It was not without danger, he warned, and of course it was absolutely illegal: Russia was at war with Poland and the war zone was closed to civilians. Clearly, Mother said, there was a lot of bribery involved but the banker had said nothing about that. She had no idea why he offered to take us along and even pay our share of expenses. Perhaps for old times' sake? We were to get ready at once and take only as much as we could carry. It was February and still extremely cold and there were repeated snowfalls. Mother and I put on two lots of underwear each and all our warmest coats, gloves and scarves; in addition Mother made me put on my brother's breeches under my skirt. So equipped we embarked, with our two bundles, in a train that took us some distance towards the front line. To travel beyond that point one had to have a special permit. That was probably where some money changed hands. Then we were led to a side track, where a few cattle trucks were being coupled to a locomotive, and were told to get into one of the cattle trucks; a few other civilians were already inside it. The doors were closed and off we went.

There was a small cast-iron stove in the middle of the truck but it threw out little heat and before long we were very cold and hungry. Now and then the train stopped, and then Red Army soldiers who were travelling on the same train came and brought some fuel and boiling water. The soldiers were friendly and joked with me and Mother and I felt much closer to them than to most of our companions. Apart from the banker and his wife we knew only one other person in the party, Mark Mazover, a Menshevik friend of Mother's who was hoping to rejoin his wife somewhere in the south. Mother said that most of our travel companions seemed to be *spekulanty* (black marketeers) and that their company made her very uneasy.

The journey took several days, but at last, late one afternoon, the train suddenly slowed and then stopped altogether in the middle of nowhere. We could hear a not too distant rat-a-tat-tat of gunfire. The soldiers hurriedly uncoupled our car, the locomotive shunted and picked up the rest of the train, then quickly steamed away to where it came from.

We were left on our own. Through the open car doors we could see nothing but rail tracks running in both directions and all around us an empty snow-covered plain, greying in the gathering dusk. Where were we? Some of the shifty-looking men in our truck seemed to know the answer to that: only a few miles to the nearest village and some few more to the town of Polotsk, on the frontier. And all of them jumped out on to the snow and made off. But they did promise to come back with a horse-sledge for us and the luggage. There was little reason to trust them, said Mother softly to Mark

Mazover, as we waited. But after a long, anxious wait, one man did return with a sledge and a horse, and the moon came up to light our way.

Our spirits rose. Quickly we piled up all our bundles on to the sledge, and the horse moved off, leaving us to trudge behind. The snow made walking difficult, our felt boots were heavy and unwieldy and our coat pockets were weighed down with all the things stuffed into them. Soon I began to lag behind, even with Mother pulling me. With every step it seemed to get darker and colder; clouds hid the moon and the frost was biting. At first Mother reasoned with me – we must keep up with the others or we would lose our way and die in the snow. But when I stopped altogether, she slapped me, for the one and only time in her life. And it worked: I walked on and soon we caught up with the others. For the last half-mile I was allowed to ride on the sledge, on top of all the bundles.

I at once fell asleep and it was only next day that I found out what had happened. We had not stopped at the village but had pushed on to Polotsk, the big town astride the River Dvina. It was this river that marked the line between the Russian and Polish forces. Most of the town was on the Polish side; on our Russian side were some deserted ware-houses and burnt-out private dwellings. In one of these, or more precisely, in its cellar, our party found refuge.

In this cellar, which we shared with the owners of the house, we spent the best part of a month, while two armies exchanged sporadic, half-hearted fire. According to our hosts, neither side was trying very hard: now and then a cease-fire would be declared and during such times people would be allowed to cross the frontier. The soldiers, they said, could be seen fraternising and exchanging food from home, on the best of terms. Meanwhile the population in the cellars was starving. Our hosts and some of their neighbours risked their lives by stealing away to villages at night to bring back food, some of which they would sell to the likes of us at exorbitant prices.

Of all this I knew little. The gunfire barely penetrated the thick walls of the cellar, but the cold and the hunger were very real. Still there was a bonus in it all for me: in the room immediately over our cellar were shelves full of books and we were told to help ourselves. To my delight there was a whole shelf of the French adventure writer, Rocombole (in Russian translation), which I immediately proceeded to devour. As far as I remember these books, like Jules Verne's before and Arsène Lupin's after, all ended with the hero over-taken by some disaster of such elemental scope that he could not possibly survive. And yet, in the very next volume there he was again, planning even more daring deeds. Mother had told me how once, when she was in prison and was completely engrossed in a Dumas novel from the prison library, the matron came with the news that she was to be released at once and how reluctant she was to leave the novel. I understood her feelings very well; there were two or three volumes of Rocombole still left on the shelf when the bombardment ceased. For that meant that a truce had been agreed and we would soon be crossing into Poland.

Our host instructed us in the rules enforced by both sides in the exchange of civilians. We were not allowed to carry mer-chandise or any letters or other printed material or photo-graphs. Cash was limited to a small amount, which had to be declared. These rules were very strictly observed, and those who failed to abide by them were shot on the spot.

Our party had shrunk a little. All the *spekulanty* had left, but we were joined by a pretty young nurse who was going to join her parents in Lithuania. Our host advised us to get as much sleep as possible that night and we were only too happy to follow his advice. But when I woke next morning Mother had gone. I jumped up in great alarm and ran to find her. I found her sitting disconsolately in front of the meagre fire in the room which served us all as a sitting-room. On her lap were the few precious possessions she had allowed herself to bring along: a photo of our whole family and one other photo, of my dead sister Galya, as well as a few letters. Now these had to be burnt and I could see how distressed she was. But I had a problem of my own. I still wore my brother's breeches under my skirt and I had stuffed both pockets of these with my poems. Yes, I was still writing poetry (inspiration was to dry up completely at the age of fourteen), and I could not face leaving my *oeuvre* behind. In taking the poems with me I had deliberately disobeyed Mother and now, as I watched her putting the letters on the fire, I decided to deceive her again. Bending down as if trying to help her, I covered the two photos with my foot as if by accident and suggested that she leave the rest to me. Glad to be spared the task of destroying what was so dear to her, she left the room. As soon as she was gone I stuffed the photos and the remaining papers into the pockets of the breeches.

A little cough from the door made me spin round and there, watching me, was the banker's wife. She looked at me long and searchingly and then, quickly shutting the door, she came close up to me. 'You know you should not be doing this, don't you? They'll shoot you.' There was nothing I could say; I could only stare mulishly. The banker's wife studied me speculatively: 'You've made up your mind, haven't you? But suppose I tell your mother?' 'No, please, please, don't tell her!' 'All right, I won't. But only if you take these two bundles as well.' I could see that the two bundles were banknotes and I knew that smuggling money was the worst offence of all, but upsetting Mother seemed to me more terrible than anything. So I took the two bundles and the banker's wife went quickly out of the room without another word.

It was a bright, frosty, sunny morning and soon our host came in and told us to hurry, as the border would be open only for a short time. We took up our bundles and marched, in a tight little cluster, down the river bank and across the ice of the river. We could see two sentry-posts facing each other, and we could also see people showing their passports and belongings for inspection. Now, suddenly, the sense of danger flooded me – not the danger of being shot by the soldier but the certainty that my deceit would be discovered by Mother. There was nothing I could do now: we were standing in a queue in front of the two huts and there was no hiding place anywhere. I saw the banker and his wife pass through the controls and walk off quickly towards the other shore. We were now close enough to the border-post to hear soldiers talking to each other. They were laughing and joking about the two sorties the week before, in which each side had raided the enemy's stores and had carried off quantities of food and drink. That seemed a kind of local sport and the scores of both sides were hotly disputed.

In fact the border guards were too busy talking to take

much notice of us and we passed through with no trouble at all. I breathed again. We walked across the ice to the opposite bank, where we could see the rest of our group talking to a tall bearded old Jew, who was offering lodgings. The price was exorbitant but we had no choice; we were glad to have a roof over our heads. As it turned out there was even a tiny fire in one of the rooms and we crouched over it gratefully. When Mother was not looking the banker's wife nudged me and I handed her the wads of banknotes. She said not a word but I saw her husband looking at her and then at me with a puzzled, unhappy expression and I realised that she had told him nothing. Horrid, horrid woman!

There was a further delay of several days. We needed special permission to board a train out of the war zone, and that depended on the goodwill of one particular Polish officer. Tall and smart, the man had been eyeing the pretty nurse. Now he made it clear that permission depended on our leaving her behind. Most of our group, it seemed, were willing to accept this. I could not rightly understand what it was all about. I went in search of the girl and found her sobbing on her bed, while Mother was furiously pacing the room: 'What can I do? I try my best but the others won't listen to me! It's like something out of Maupassant!' Whatever were they doing to that nice, pretty girl who had become my friend? When we left next morning, without the nurse, Mother was still seething and I was very sad.

Our next stop was Vilna, where the group dispersed. In Vilna we used to have many relatives, on both sides of the family.

But now, as we trudged from one address to the next, we found them all gone. We learned of the dreadful fate that had befallen Svenciany Jews during the Civil War. The district had been devastated by marauding armies and armed bands. Each time another of them arrived it looted everything in sight, horses and carriages, food and clothes. When a band of Greens arrived (or was it Reds or some other colour?), their leaders called together the elders of the Jewish community, made them surrender anything of value they still possessed and then took them, with their wives and children, in cattle trucks a few miles out of town. There they dragged the men out and shot them, in front of their families. Then they galloped away. Among those shot were relatives of Father's. Luckily, young cousin Joseph had a few days earlier gone to Vilna and was staying with our grandparents. But his even younger sister Dora witnessed it all. It was the first horrific chapter in a life that was later to take her into Soviet and Nazi camps.

Only one address in Vilna yielded any results: there we learned that Father had indeed been in Vilna at the time of his mother's death, but had left soon after and gone to Warsaw or perhaps to Vienna. 'It had better be Warsaw,' said Mother. 'Our money will never stretch further.' But Warsaw brought disappointment. Father had been there only briefly. Unable to make his way back to Petrograd, he had gone to his brother in Vienna. Where were we to go and what were we to do? Warsaw was a miserable, bedraggled city that spring of 1920. Slush was ankle-deep on the sidewalks of the Marshalkowska, formerly celebrated as one of the most elegant main streets in the world. On almost every corner there were soldiers, stamping their feet and warming their hands at braziers of hot coals. Their rifles were stacked wigwam-style right on the corner so that we had to step off into the road to pass them. A cold wind was blowing loose paper and refuse about in the thoroughfare. We walked slowly along the street towards the Old Town, though we knew nobody there, or elsewhere in Warsaw. How were we to get money for the tickets to Vienna or indeed for lodgings in Warsaw? I could see that Mother was at the end of her tether. She was coughing painfully as we walked aimlessly, dragging our feet in the slush.

Then, all of a sudden, Mother stopped, bent down and picked something up from the ground. 'No questions, please, no talking.' We walked on but I noticed that she was walking just a little bit faster. When we had gone a little way she explained that she had picked up an earring with what looked like a diamond in it. In ordinary circumstances, she said, we should take it to the police but our circumstances were not ordinary and our need was very great, and anyway the fool of a woman who wore diamond earrings these days deserved no better than to lose them! It would be difficult to convert our find into ready money but we would try; we would go to the Jewish quarter in the Old Town and find a small jeweller to buy it from us.

That proved quite difficult. Most shops were closed, their windows boarded up; and there were very few people in the streets to enquire of. In the end we found a shop that seemed to show a dim light behind the closed shutters. We passed and repassed it several times before Mother plucked up courage to knock at the door. There was no answer so she knocked again. Then the door was opened, just a crack, by an old Jew who surveyed us in silence for a few moments and then waved us in. Carefully locking the door behind us, he invited us, in Yiddish, to sit down. Mother spoke Yiddish fluently and she now told him our entire history, ending with the finding of the earring. Would he buy it from her or at least lend her enough for two third-class tickets to Vienna?

The old man looked at us thoughtfully. Did we know what the Polish police would do to him should the earring be traced to him? They would say he was a receiver of stolen goods, a dirty Jew, and let him rot in prison. And did we know that no woman could travel unmolested on Polish trains, crowded with drunken soldiery? 'However,' and at that we looked up hopefully, 'a way must be found . . .' He would not try to sell the jewel for a long time, he would hide it; in the meantime he would get us two first-class tickets for Vienna in the international wagon-lits. And without waiting for Mother's thanks he called his son, a robust young man, and told him to go at once to the main railway station and get the tickets. We could wait in the shop and dry our wet shoes; and, perhaps, eat a bite? We both cried a little with relief and gratitude. And when his son returned with the tickets, the old man told him to take us to the station, see us to our compartment and give the conductor a fat tip to draw down the blinds and lock us in. All of which the son did, with a great deal of kindness, much care and thoughtfulness, steering us safely through the crowded station and even procuring for us a little food for the journey.

Our two beds were freshly made up with spotless, crisp linen. There were clean towels and soap on the washbasin. Everything was shining and incredibly luxurious. We sat there as in a dream, not quite trusting our luck. Only when the train moved out of the station could we relax. Even then, we were almost too tired to eat or sleep. But in the end the lure of the soft beds won and we were asleep the moment our heads touched the pillows.

Next morning we were in Vienna.

I I

WE DID NOT STAY in Vienna above six months; we did not feel welcome there. Uncle Lyova was truly glad to see us: he and Father were very close and long ago he had himself been in love with Mother. But his wife and three daughters were less welcoming. They found us embarrassing in our shabby clothes and down-at-heel shoes. Our hair was not properly groomed and our hands were not manicured; we did not fit into their elegant drawing-room, nor did we feel relaxed in it. I hardly dared to sit down on the chintzy sofa or move about among the fragile little tables, the tall lamps, the glass vases with flowers. On every count I felt a proper savage. We all felt much happier when we moved to a furnished room a few streets away.

Everybody was telling us, in a sepulchral kind of voice, that Vienna was no longer the glittering city it had been: it was drab and starved and all gaiety had gone out of it. But to us Vienna was still a horn of plenty: there was food in the stores, bread and cakes of every kind in the bakeries, clothes and shoes and trinkets in the fashion shops. And no queues anywhere! And when we went into a large and lavishly appointed patisserie we even could buy a pischinger torte. This exquisite Viennese speciality had always been included in the annual New Year's parcel that Uncle Lyova used to send us in my early childhood years, and it was, in my opinion, the greatest of all treats. So what were these people complaining about? 'All is relative,' said Father indulgently, 'to them this is misery.' While in furnished lodgings we ate every day at a small restaurant, always the same lunch: a Wiener schnitzel with fried potatoes and green peas, while the elderly waiter told us age-old Viennese jokes. It was my idea of absolute bliss.

We could see, of course, that the streets were almost as dirty and full of litter as in Warsaw and the houses needed repair and new paint almost as much as in Petrograd. However, there was much to be seen and every day we three went out exploring. St Stephen's Cathedral was the first Gothic building I had ever seen and I was awe-struck by its vastness and its gauntness; Russian churches, round, ornate, truly motherly, spoke more intimately to me. The spacious gardens of Schönbrunn were handsome but could anything compare with St Petersburg? That I could never accept.

No, it was a discovery of quite another kind that filled my days in Vienna with a glow. For the first time in my life I felt that I belonged to a proper family. As we walked, hand in hand, the three of us, through Vienna streets, I walked on clouds. I had Father all for myself and was not afraid that tomorrow or next week he would again disappear. As we walked and he explained to us the history or the purpose of the buildings and places, I listened to his voice more than to his words. So this was my father – how little I knew him! But soon I knew that we were and would always be the closest of beings; we were made of the same stuff, cut from the same cloth. And not only because, alone in our family, we were both fair and had bluish-green eyes – we were spiritually citizens of the same planet. My dark-haired, dark-eyed Mother was of quite a different make, dearly as I loved her. Of course I really knew neither of them very well and it was only years later that I came to understand them properly.

Meanwhile, while we walked, Father and Mother talked of our future. Father said that political life in Austria was moribund, and Mother, having visited some of her old friends among the Austrian socialists, agreed with him: her friends were most depressed. Father also said that there were no jobs to be found and that he could not remain his brother's pensioner forever. They decided to try their luck in Germany.

While in Vienna we went to see a doctor about Mother's illness. It turned out, fortunately, that there was nothing basically wrong with her; nothing that good food and rest would not cure. And indeed she recovered quickly. It was my health, on the other hand, that suddenly created problems: eating more and better food after those years of near-starvation, I shot up like a toadstool and apparently there was not enough 'building material' in me to sustain such rapid growth. Neither my bones nor my inner organs could keep up with it and as a result I might become a complete invalid. But, said the Viennese doctor, there was a famous orthopaedic clinic in Berlin, which would no doubt be able to help me.

We packed up and went, after saying a grateful farewell to Uncle Lyova.

In the early twenties, when we arrived, Berlin was awash with Russian refugees, thousands of them: remnants of the defeated White armies, ruined bankers and industrialists, members of political parties from monarchists to socialists, university professors, writers, poets, painters, actors, musicians. Most of them were never integrated into German life; many did not even learn the language. They formed a kind of Russian microcosm in which Russians worked for Russians: university professors taught in schools for Russian children, former Imperial Army generals and officers ran or worked in Russian restaurants. One of our friends peddled – literally carried in an ice-box on his back – *smetana* (a delicious kind of soured cream), cream cheese and other produce 'in the Russian style', all prepared by his wife in their tiny kitchen. Many had no jobs at all and subsisted on Lord knows what; many had only one threadbare suit and one pair of shoes. But somehow they survived. And émigré cultural life flourished. Novelists like Vladimir Nabokov, poets like Ivan Bunin published in Russian-language newspapers and journals. The historian Gessen edited and published a voluminous *Chronicle of the Revolution*, to which many émigrés, including Mother, contributed. There were concerts and poetry readings, dripping with nostalgia for the lost homeland. There were also innumerable clubs and circles, including a very active Menshevik Club with at least a hundred members. The Germans, defeated and impoverished as they were, coped splendidly with that unexpected human flood. They even provided much material aid.

We were among the lucky ones. Father was offered a job with one of the Soviet foreign trade organisations. Soviet Russia was desperately short of people with professional qualifications and foreign languages and, though they were not officially authorised to do so, individual directors were happy to employ Russian refugees, particularly Mensheviks, whom they knew they could trust. So it came about that many Mensheviks held important positions in various Soviet organisations. In the end, of course, orders would come from Moscow to sack all Mensheviks, but that lay in the future.

For the present my parents could afford to rent a sizeable apartment in Grünewald and, moreover, to send me to an excellent, and expensive, orthopaedic clinic. I had daily treatment for almost a year, to correct a curvature of the spine and to strengthen my limbs generally. It was most unpleasant – being stretched and hung up by the neck. I was also supplied with orthopaedic boots with metal supports, as my legs would not carry me. That first year I could hardly walk for more than a quarter of an hour at a time. Eventually I recovered and by the age of fifteen I could lay aside the tiresome boots and say goodbye to the various instruments of torture in the clinic. I was by then a tall strapping girl with a huge mop of red hair, and the street boys would run after me shouting: *'Das Mädchen mit dem Löwenhaupt!'* (the girl with a lion's head), which was the title of a serialised novel in the weekly *Berliner Illustrierte Zeitung.*

In Berlin my parents met up again with their Menshevik comrades. Soon Martov himself arrived and came to stay with us for several months, until his sister Lydia and her husband Fyodr Dan came too, and the three of them moved into an apartment of their own.

Originally Martov had been a close friend and associate of Lenin. Together they had helped to introduce Marxism into Russia; together they had helped to found the Russian Social Democratic Party. But the splitting of that party into Bolsheviks, under Lenin, and Mensheviks, under Martov, was inevitable. Martov saw that the only kind of regime that could emerge from Lenin's style of leadership would be a one-party regime supported by terror. He also understood that such a regime must infallibly betray the humane ideals of socialism and bring untold suffering upon the masses it purported to serve.

Now Martov had come to Germany to attend the congress of the German Independent Social Democrats at Halle, in August 1920. He delivered there one of his most incisive attacks on Lenin's policies. The German Independents, like so many other left-wing Western socialists, tended to idealise the Bolsheviks at that time, but Martov's speech made a deep impression on them. Breitscheid and Rudolf Hilferding and many others among the leaders became more critical of Soviet Russia. Martov had intended to return to Russia after the congress; but it soon became clear that while the Russian government had been willing enough to let him go, he was not to be allowed back. In fact the Bolsheviks were very happy to have got rid of their most persistent critic.

There was also the matter of Martov's health. Early in his life – probably in exile in the swampy Turukhansk region of northern Siberia – he had contracted a tubercular throat. It had affected his vocal chords so severely that he could only speak in a croak. He needed specialist treatment and care. In the few remaining years before his death in April 1923, he went repeatedly to sanatoria in the country but there seemed little hope of recovery. His mind was, however, as clear as ever and he developed a feverish activity during the spells of relatively good health.

In Russia the Menshevik Party was forced to go underground. The party press was banned, party leaders and rank-and-file members were imprisoned, their representatives were expelled from the soviets. Outside Russia Martov was able to found the Menshevik Delegation Abroad and its organ the *Socialist Courier*. Mother was much involved with this Russian journal. In fact at first she carried out, almost single-handedly, all the chores involved in its publication – travelling once a month to Thuringia, where she had located a printing press with Russian type, then collecting and distributing the printed copies. And the *Socialist Courier* flourished: it became known to scholars throughout the world as an invaluable source of reliable information on Soviet Russia. Moreover, it survived well into the 1960s.

The Delegation Abroad at first consisted of only three members, Martov, Abramovich and Mother. But soon it was joined by the many members of the Menshevik Central Committee who had been expelled from Russia. Our home became the centre of the Menshevik colony. Not only were the regular editorial meetings of the *Socialist Courier* held there – in the evenings many of the Menshevik families gathered round our vast dining-room table. We often had as many as twenty guests; on my fourteenth birthday there were forty.

My particular friends were the Dans, the Abramoviches and Boris Nikolaevsky. The Dans I knew from Minusinsk; they remained my closest friends. With Nikolaevsky I had an uncle–niece relationship, in fact he called himself my adopted uncle. A giant of a man, with huge arms and hands, and with the face of a Kalmyk idol – high cheekbones, flat nose, slit eyes – he was surprisingly gentle. Abramovich took a keen interest in the children of our colony. He even tried to introduce me to socialism through the writings of the founding fathers – Saint-Simon, Fourier, Blanqui, Proudhon, and of course Marx and Engels. I read the texts he gave me with interest, but they did not have the intended effect. On the contrary, when I returned them to him I said that I had no wish at all to devote my life to any political cause, socialist or other.

There was another Menshevik in Berlin, the most famous of them all: Pavel Borisovich Axelrod, who along with Lenin and Martov had been an editor of *Iskra*. Originally Axelrod had acquired his education by a curious route. Under a decree of the tsarist government, a certain percentage of the Jewish boys in any town or village in the Pale of Settlement had to attend a Russian school instead of a synagogue school. Pious Jews could not easily stomach this, so a bizarre kind of corruption developed, with rich Jews bribing poor Jews to send their sons to Russian schools, so as not to have to send their own. Pavel Axelrod, who came from a poor family, was a beneficiary of this practice. Now, old and infirm, he lived in comparative isolation, did not belong to the Delegation and took no part in editing the *Socialist Courier*. But he was still the grand old man of Menshevism, venerated and loved by all. Mother often took me to visit him, and he and I became firm friends.

I recall a congress of the Second International in Hamburg. The Menshevik Party, which was affiliated to the International, sent a substantial delegation to the congress; Mother represented Menshevik women. Pavel Axelrod was invited, and I was attached to him as a kind of honorary nurse. While the meeting went on inside the great hall of the Vierjahreszeiten Hotel, he and I sat under a large tree outside. I had to see to it that he was neither too hot nor too cold, and to fetch him cups of coffee from the hotel. We chatted together, mainly about the celebrities who passed us on their way to the hall: the Webbs, Ramsay MacDonald, Paul Faure. Many of them stopped to shake hands with the old man: he was very popular in the international socialist community. Once a tall, white-haired patriarch stopped to have a long chat with him. Pavel Borisovich was obviously very pleased. 'It is a great privilege for you to meet this man,' he said to me, 'it was he who financed Karl Marx's first International.' 'And this,' he hugged me, 'is my adopted granddaughter.' I don't, I'm afraid, recall the name of the man, only that he was a Dutch plantation owner from Java.

But of all the Mensheviks in Berlin it was Martov who attracted me most powerfully. I fell for him when he first came to stay with us in Berlin and all the party meetings took place in our drawing-room. I was allowed to sit in at those meetings, provided I did not disturb anyone, and I crouched on the floor at Martov's feet as quiet as a mouse. What was there in him to captivate a thirteen-year-old? Certainly not his looks – stooping shoulders, lame leg, scraggy beard, eyes hidden by glasses. It was, rather, something inside him – a quick, impatient mind, certainly, but also real passion, an unquenchable inner fire. To me he seemed the most vital force among all the Mensheviks, and I worshipped him with all the fervour of my adolescent heart.

I was not prepared for his death, even though Mother had taken me several times to see him in the sanatorium, and we could see him getting weaker each time. When he died, I was shaken as nothing had shaken me before; I could not accept the finality of the loss. I was still dazed when I went with my parents to the crematorium. The big round hall was full of people. All the Mensheviks were there, and also German and other foreign socialists and many other Russian exiles. I was too distressed to listen to the endless speeches; all my senses were glued to that small coffin on the raised dais that stood before a dark curtain. And when that curtain was raised and the coffin began to glide slowly away, I was seized by such panic and horror that I turned and ran, ran through the crowd towards the doors. I was blinded by tears, I stumbled and dodged, until, all at once, my path was blocked by a huge figure and I was seized and pressed to a broad chest. It was Boris Nikolaevsky and he, too, was crying; and so we clung together shaken by sobs, until he turned and led me out into the garden. I walked home by myself, not wanting to wait for Mother and Father.

Meanwhile Mother was fretting about my schooling. By all formal standards I was, at thirteen, a complete ignoramus. That is, I had begun reading at the age of four and had read voraciously ever since, but I had had no sustained teaching. Mine had been a free-roaming, unfettered childhood and, as Mother soon found, it was not possible, at that late stage, to fit me into any kind of school, particularly not into a German one. Her first attempt was to put me into a boarding school. The idea was that I would learn good German as well as acquire good manners. I did learn German and much besides, as the teaching was very good; but I hated every minute of it. My only happy memory was learning to play the piano. My teacher was a kindly elderly lady who had been a pupil of Schnabel, and I still remember how jubilant and proud I was when she judged me competent enough to play from 'Mozart operas for four hands' with her, or an easy piece of Beethoven! But this did not quite compensate for my other miseries, and after six months Mother yielded to my entreaties and I left the school. My only regret was that this also put an end to my musical education.

After this I was put, in quick succession, into a *klassisches Gymnasium* (with Latin and Greek) and then into a *Realschule* (mainly science), but I simply could not tolerate the restraint – *Ordnung* – of a German school. So what was to become of me? Fortunately an unexpected solution presented itself: a new Russian school was being opened in Berlin, with an excellent and liberal teaching staff, as an alternative to the existing Russian school, which was very reactionary. After an interview with the director of this new school it was agreed that I should be coached at home in order to enter the highest grade or class a year hence.

My coach turned out to be a quite exceptional teacher, and I worked very willingly for him. The routine was hard – I sat at my desk the whole day, leaving it only for meals and short walks around the block on which Mother insisted. One day at lunch she complained that a boxer had installed his training ring on the ground floor of our house immediately below our flat, so that everything shook and rattled when he trained; and there were posh cars coming and going all day long, disturbing our quiet street. That was indeed news! I soon winkled out that the boxer was one of the top heavy-weights, Hans Breitenstätter; in addition he was very good-looking, and most of the cars that waited in our street belonged to his female admirers. One day when I was on one of my round-the-block walks, I saw him jogging alongside me. 'Do you mind timing me?' he said, handing me a large watch. And so I did repeatedly from then on, jogging easily alongside him, much to the annoyance of the ladies in the cars. I didn't tell Mother about all this, and she was pleased that my walks were becoming somewhat longer.

Early in the 1920s my brother Danya arrived in Berlin. He had been 'missing' since 1918. In the summer of that year, that is when he was about fourteen, Mother had sent him to Tomsk. But soon Tomsk was cut off by the Civil War and we lost all trace of him for several years. It appeared later that during the Civil War he had been first a cattle minder, on a large farm, and then a partisan fighting against the Whites in the Siberian forests. When the war was over, he, with three other young partisans, was selected as good officer material, to go to the Red Army Officers' School in Petrograd. There he spent many of his days off searching for us, but in vain, until one day he was stopped in the street by a complete stranger: 'You look so like Eva Broido, could you be related?' Once this link was established, word was sent to us in Berlin, wheels were set in motion and he soon joined us. I found it hard to reconcile my memory of a schoolboy brother with the tall, lanky youth that he now was. Nor did I have much chance to get closer to him: he was keen to catch up on his studies and, once he enrolled at the *Technische Hochschule* (technological university), he had little time for his kid sister.

We had another unexpected visitor that year. One day a young man with a small bundle over his shoulder and a violin-case under his arm arrived and introduced himself as a distant cousin of Mother's from Svenciany. He was a typical *shtetl* fiddler. He explained that he was walking through Europe – France next, then perhaps Spain, then with luck to North Africa. He had no more luggage than he could carry about with him, and he earned his keep by playing his fiddle at street corners. He was a small man, almost a dwarf, but when he tucked his fiddle under his chin he seemed to grow. And when we asked him to play for us, he played a Jewish lament so full of grief that I have never forgotten it. He stayed with us a few days, then went on his way. I often wondered where he ended up.

When at last I was ready to go to school – to the highest class of the new Russian school – I didn't hate it, as I had hated my previous schools; I loved it. All our teachers were of the highest calibre. We were taught mathematics by a Mongolian, Babagay Zurna, who endowed his subject with such poetry and beauty that I was enthralled. History was an unending adventure, literature a source of lifelong delight.

Philosophy and logic were taught by a former professor at Moscow University, Pavel Karsavin, brother of the famous ballerina Tamara Karsavina. Towards the end of the school year, when the time came for revision, I joined forces with his daughter Irina, and he offered to cram us both. I went to their home each evening. Then he took us through one subject after another – quite ruthlessly, no matter how we drooped. But at the end of each session he rewarded us with a spell of poetry reading in Latin, Russian or German. He was a fascinating man, attractive in looks and still more in personality. And I owe him much. At the end of the year we were all examined by a mixed board of German and Russian examiners, and those who passed were entitled to study at a German university. I surprised myself by passing with good marks.

Sometime during that momentous year I acquired a pupil, or more precisely a 'talking partner': a young professor from Princeton, in Berlin for a spell of research, who wanted to improve his German by conversation. He came twice a week and we talked, and sometimes went for a walk, still talking, and sometimes went to the Palais de Danse in the Tauentzien Strasse, where we did not talk but danced. He turned out to be an excellent and enthusiastic dancer. His style of dancing was very different from the tame fox-trotting fashionable in Berlin. No such restraint for my American; a tall, thin man with long legs, he fairly swept me around the dance floor, holding me loosely but strongly so that I felt I was flying in one of those Luna Park fairground wheels that thrust you into space from a central axis. To me it was a revelation, like learning to swim or to fly. We danced wonderfully well together and the precision and rhythm of our joint move-ment gave me a sense of freedom and mastery that I had never felt before. Dancing had acquired a new dimension, akin to the fulfilment and pleasure derived from writing poetry or, I imagined, composing music.

Once the examinations were over Mother began to fret about my career. She was determined to have me study at a university, all the more because she had not had a university education herself. Besides, Russian radical women had fought so hard for the right to study, it seemed a shame not to avail oneself of the chance to do so. I felt rather lukewarm about it, especially as I had no idea of what I wanted to study. But when she suggested, in all innocence, that I might like to study in France, perhaps in Paris, at the Sorbonne, I was enthusiastic. Mother was convinced that leaving home at an early age, as she herself had done, was good for the character. She had no idea to what perils she was exposing me. Strangely enough, for all my lack of worldly wisdom, I had a somewhat clearer idea of those perils, but that was precisely what attracted me. And so it was decided – I was to go to Paris, to study at the Sorbonne.

I2

And now I was in Paris. Mother took me there herself to see that I was properly settled. The Russian *émigré* colony in Paris was almost as large as the colony in Berlin. The best Russian-language newspaper was published there, and there were many Russian restaurants. But Mensheviks were very few. One, a friend of Mother's, was on the staff of the socialist newspaper *Le Populaire*, and she asked him to pay me my monthly allowance. To my delight, she also bought me some very nice French clothes.

But where to find me suitable lodgings? Students, we were told, usually stayed in small hotels on the Left Bank, and we soon found a tiny room in a hotel in the rue Lacepède, next to the Jardin des Plantes – which, oddly, turned out to be, not the Botanical Gardens but the Zoo.

Mother was uneasy: could she really leave me alone,

among strangers, in a hotel? The problem was quickly resolved, in a most unexpected manner. The day before she was due to leave for Berlin, as we were sitting in my room sorting out my belongings and discussing my future, there was a knock on the door. '*Entrez!*' I said, in my still hesitant French – and the door was opened by a very tall, very handsome young man. 'Eva Gordón?' he asked. 'I have a letter from home to say you are in Paris. I'm so glad to have found you!' It transpired that the young giant was a medical student in his second year and that he was a native of Svenciany. Back home, he explained, Mother was a local heroine, a famous revolutionary whom the people were proud to call their own. 'In our backwater, you understand, there are few heroes, and people are still talking about the intrepid young woman who was Eva Gordón.' But how did he find us? Nothing easier: there were some Jewish families living in the working-class districts of Paris who kept in touch with home and with each other and who always knew who was coming and who was going. We all three saw the humour of the situation: here was the 'famous revolutionary', who had prided herself on her skill in evading the tsarist police – and nothing was easier than to trace her from Berlin to a small hotel in Paris! Anyway, here he was, the young man, eager to help. Mother was much relieved and gladly entrusted me to his care. Now she could leave Paris with a light heart.

It was of course imprudent of Mother to leave her seventeen-year-old daughter in the care of a handsome and practically unknown young man, but in the event she was proved right. The young man felt honour bound not to try to seduce me, and for my part I was not yet ready for any deep involvement. Abrasha and I became the best of friends. During the week he was busy with his studies, but every Sunday he called for me and together we explored the city. As neither of us had much money we found a good and cheap way of getting about: Paris buses charged the same fare whatever distance you went, so we always went all the way to the terminus, there to walk about and lunch on a snack from a street stall. So we got to know all the ends of Paris, one *porte* after another – and how different they all were! Sometimes we ended up at the home of a friend of Abrasha's, a Jewish tailor who lived near the Porte St Martin. There we were made welcome and given a huge meal. The tailor, a small, wiry man, never left off working even when he talked to us; he could not afford to. His wife was a quiet motherly little woman, whom I suspected of washing and mending Abrasha's clothes.

Abrasha never introduced me to any of his fellow students because 'they could not be trusted'. Most of them were as poor as he was himself and, as he explained, the height of their ambitions was to collect some insurance money after an accident: perhaps a slight contretemps with a cruising taxi, not too serious, no bones broken, and not much money, just enough for a new suit or a pair of new shoes. Poor Abrasha, he tried it too, but the taxi was going too fast and he landed in hospital. I did not learn whether he bought himself a new suit, for by that time I had left Paris.

I had only one other friend in my early days in Paris, and he was the nephew of a couple Mother knew. He took me out sometimes, most usually to a café on the Boulevard St Michel, the Boul'Mich, where we sat for hours at a table with many of his friends and their *petites amies*, the *midinettes*. The girls were very nice to me and I thought them charming. Sometimes we all went dancing at the *bal musette*; it was noisy and smoky and crowded but so jolly (and quite unlike its German counterpart in Berlin). Equally crowded and smoky was the local cinema, where we went to see Douglas Fairbanks and Mary Pickford and the Gish sisters and countless French serial adventure films which we never missed, week after week.

But my greatest pleasure was to walk round Paris by myself, as I used to do in Petrograd. On my daily morning walk I passed through the delightful Place Mouffetard, which forever after remained my favourite French square, and its adjoining market in the Rue Mouffetard; and then across the Rue St Jacques and around the Panthéon. I came to love the tortured iron chairs in the Luxembourg Gardens, wet after rain; the cavernous arches around the Odéon; the teeming market in the Rue de Seine; and the miracle of the two-tier embankments, cobbled and empty below and crammed with book stalls and book hunters above. The Left Bank seemed inexhaustible. I wandered around aimlessly, going here and there in search of new wonders – anywhere in fact, but to the Sorbonne.

The Sorbonne was a great disappointment; too fast and too impersonal. After one paid the fees and received a student card, nobody took any notice of you, nobody advised you or directed your studies or monitored your progress. For a little while I tried to find a course that would interest me – I was still teetering between literature and philosophy – but couldn't find one. I went to several lectures by famous professors – these were public lectures and I could have gone to them even without paying my fees. Really, I was wasting my time. But the Sorbonne became largely irrelevant when, half-way through the academic year, I met Alexandra

Alexandrovna Exter, the Russian Constructivist painter and was fired with ambition to become a painter myself.

I don't remember how and where I met Alexandra Alexandrovna but I do remember that I immediately fell under her spell. Or perhaps not quite immediately. At first sight she seemed to be a typical middle-aged Russian woman (though she claimed Greek descent on her father's side), rather broad and somewhat stolid. But at second sight one became aware of an exceptional strength behind her placidity. She reminded me of Nekrasov's poem 'There are women in Russian villages' – she was a powerful woman, she had majesty. She once told me that when she first came to Paris, she was befriended by Fernand Léger, and he said to her, and of her: '*Les femme russes sont des négresses blanches.*' That describes her beautifully.

In Russia her rise to fame had been meteoric. She had begun her painting career in Kiev but by 1916 she was in Moscow, designing for the Kamerny Theatre under its famous director Tayrov. For all the arts in Russia this was a time of daring innovation. Among painters names such as Malevich, Tatlin, Rodchenko came to the fore, and among poets names such as Mayakovsky and Yesenin. The theatre too was undergoing revolutionary changes. Directors like Meyerhold, Vakhtangov, Tayrov called for revolutionary designers. Alexandra Exter established the Constructivist style in the Russian theatre. She broke with the realistic set, banished the backcloth and opened the stage up to free movement and light. She erected platforms on different levels, with ladders and steps leading in different directions.

She experimented with coloured lights on white and grey-robed actors. The success of her work in Moscow was prodigious. In 1918 the Bolshevik Commissar for Arts and Education, Anatoly Lunacharsky, declared that the Romanovs having been ousted, new tsars were now placed on the throne of Russia: tsar Nikolay Rodchenko and tsaritsa Alexandra Exter.

The enthusiasm was short-lived. Very soon the Bolshevik government turned against all innovation in the arts. As Socialist Realism was imposed from above, the atmosphere became stifling. Those who would not conform were marginalised. Only film directors who were prepared to serve as government propagandists flourished. Mayakovsky and Yesenin killed themselves and Alexandra Exter left Russia for ever.

She had been abroad before. In 1908 she had met Picasso, Braque and the Italian Futurists. She had travelled widely in Italy, where Venice became what it was to remain for the rest of her life, her favourite subject for painting and drawing. For some years she had also kept a studio in Paris. Now, in 1924, she settled in France for good.

I don't know when or how she met and married Georges Nekrasov. In Russia he had been a popular operetta star, a matinée idol, but by the time I met him he had lost most of his good looks, though he still had a certain elegance and much charm. In Paris he no longer worked in the theatre, but he was devoted to his Asya and quite content to be her cook and man of all work. It was she who was the breadwinner, though she too found it hard enough to get work.

When I met them in 1925/6, they were living in one of the studio houses in the Rue Broca, near Metro Glacière, within walking distance of Montparnasse. Their flat consisted of a roomy entrance hall which served as a dining-room and which opened on the left into a small kitchen and a smaller bedroom, while ahead lay the huge studio, with a high ceiling and a gallery running, half-way up, along one whole side.

When Mother heard that I was chucking the Sorbonne and was going to study painting she came to Paris in great alarm. But she simmered down when she met Alexandra Alexandrovna. In fact she took greatly to her – they were both dominant personalities, both had a quality of quiet power, and they recognised themselves in each other. Mother no longer objected; it was agreed that I would become apprenticed to Alexandra Alexandrovna and that I would move into her studio house. For a fixed monthly fee I would get full board and tuition. I was to have the small bedroom, while my hosts slept on the gallery. Alexandra Alexandrovna frankly admitted that the monthly cheque from my parents would be her only secure source of income. Otherwise her earnings were, to say the least, erratic: she had quite a repu-tation as a teacher but there were many ebbs in the number of pupils, while as a painter and theatrical designer she had to compete with far too many other expatriate Russians.

I was unbelievably happy in the Rue Broca. I was made to feel like a daughter of the family and fitted comfortably into the daily routine. In the mornings Asya (as I also learnt to call her) usually went out early, to browse in the painters' shops in Montparnasse or the art galleries in the Rue de la Boétie. In the meantime Georgik and I cleaned the house and fed the pets – the beautiful black Persian cat and the mischievous fox terrier. The large expanse of the studio floor, uncarpeted, was swept by us with two brooms, to the tunes of Georgik's earlier operetta successes: 'Now we go to Maxim's', Can-Can and the like. While Georgik sang in his slightly cracked voice, we wielded our brooms in unison, moving sideways in the manner of chorus girls and kicking our legs as high as they would go. It was great fun. The terrier snapped at our ankles but the cat disgustedly stalked out of the house, to return in the evening for a good long sleep. After sweeping and dusting and setting tables and chairs for Asya's classes, Georgik departed for the market.

When Asya returned, the serious business of the day began. She ran two kinds of courses: painting proper and applied art (fashion design, embroidery and so on). I was to take part in both. Every morning I helped her to set out paper, pencils, brushes, oils, gouaches and other materials on the long tables and to check on a list how many pupils were coming. Her own work, painting or drawing for her own pleasure or – Glory be! – for a commission, had to be fitted in between classes or in the evenings. At such times I was banned from the studio and the door was firmly shut.

My happiest moments were when Asya was neither working nor teaching and I was alone with her in the studio. All around us, on the walls, were hung her oils of Venice. These were rather dark canvasses – the stagnant waters of the narrow canals lapping around the innumerable black poles that stuck upwards like a leafless forest. I think she saw Venice as a decaying city, dying yet incredibly beautiful. Asya did not speak to me about her own paintings, but she spoke often about the art of painting in general and more particularly about the art of seeing. How to see objects, people, streets and buildings as shapes or structures. 'When you walk down the street,' she said, 'see the lines of both sides converging in the distance, lines of street lamps or trees diminishing and melting into the same distance, see houses and roofs thrusting upwards. Find the basic shape and movement of all things before you see the surface, details, cobbles under your feet, tiles on the roofs and light suffusing them all. Strip all visible things to the skeleton. And when you then start to interpret, to translate what you have seen into the language of painting, to put some flesh on the skeleton so to speak, you will find a bewildering mass of data from which to choose. There is an almost unlimited number of ways in which you can approach the task.'

I began to understand the principles underlying the different styles of painting. It was only a first tentative peep, the first insight into what constitutes the art of painting, but even that immeasurably enriched my appreciation of it. Alexandra Exter was a great creative artist, and just living alongside her taught me much about the tortuous ways of creation. She was also an inspiring teacher and I was an enthusiastic pupil. I had a place of my own in the studio at the smallest of the trestle tables, which was also used for storing paper, paint etc. And there I spent many enthralling hours either building up and then drawing or painting still-lifes (my favourite medium was gouache) or working an abstract composition of lines and shapes. Asya encouraged me to go to picture galleries and look at paintings. I was particularly impressed, among the modern abstract painters, by Amédée Ozenfant, and was forever drawing racks of plates and rows of jugs in his style.

Asya also gave a course on theatrical costume design. I remember one occasion during that course when she grew particularly eloquent on the danger of using stereotyped ideas of national styles. Just then she was interrupted by the arrival of a visitor. It was her close friend Bronislava Nijinska, sister of the famous dancer and a dancer and choreographer in her own right. She was almost entirely deaf, but she could hear Asya's clear, slow speech. On this occasion Asya explained to her that the class was discussing national styles and asked Bronislava to 'dance Egyptian' to us. The dancer thought for a minute and then began to move. It was a miracle, unforgettable – here was an ancient Egyptian woman come to life.

At meal times it was mainly Georgik who talked; Asya was often preoccupied or just tired, but his chatter soon cheered her up. Georgik was a vivid raconteur and regaled us with scenes from the neighbourhood market where he bought our food. The fat butcher's wife, the vegetable lady, the poultry man – they all came to life, complete with their various accents and typical gestures. Who could resist the charm of those cameo performances? Asya relaxed. Georgik and I basked in her good humour, the black cat went to sleep on his chair at the table and the ceiling lamp shone on what seemed to me to be the perfect family idyll.

Sometimes in the evenings we went to Montparnasse to meet friends. Russian painters and writers preferred the quieter Flore to the more popular and crowded Rotonde or the Dôme, and Asya and Georgik had many friends there. There were Goncharova and Larionov, the Annenkovs, the Ehrenburgs, all Asya's artistic connections from her Moscow years. The writer and journalist Ilya Ehrenburg, whose wife had been a pupil of Asya's in Kiev, had *his* table at the Flore, at which nobody else ever dared to sit.

The Ehrenburgs lived in a hotel in the Avenue de Maine, where many other Russians also lived. The proprietor was a

Jew from Odessa married to a French woman. He was quite uneducated but tremendously proud of the fact that so many learned people, artists and writers, stayed at his hotel. He did not mind that they were usually in arrears with the rent, but his wife did, and they were for ever rowing about it. Ehrenburg was fond of telling about one such row which he had overheard: 'You don't understand,' the husband was saying in a voice of infinite patience, as if it were not the first time he was saying it, 'what is money, what is it worth compared with fame? Why, one of these days there will be a bronze plaque fixed to the outer wall of this very hotel, saying, in large letters: HERE LIVED EHRENBURG WITH THE WIFE OF BABEL'. 'Mrs Babel,' the wife of the writer Isaak Babel, did indeed live at the same hotel, but she was not amused by this story – she detested Ehrenburg.

I was sometimes sent by Asya to collect or return a book or just to take a note to the Ehrenburgs. Theirs was, I found, a very strange ménage. They lived in separate rooms, on different floors, and while she was always immaculately neat and chic, he was not just untidy but unwashed. Their rooms were no less different: whereas hers was tidy, his was dirty, with books and papers everywhere, his famous pipes all over his desk and thick pipe smoke darkening the air. Once when I met his wife on the stairs and asked her to give Ehrenburg a book I had brought, she refused to do so: 'I never enter his room, I shudder at the thought – you give it to him yourself, thank you!'

Meanwhile my hopes of becoming a painter suffered a setback. I was an enthusiastic pupil but that, said Asya, was not enough; it was not that I was without talent; I was, in fact, talented enough to work in applied art, such as fashion design, but not enough to become a major painter. She did not want me, she said, to be one of the mediocrities that crowded the world of art. It was better to face the truth and lay aside great ambitions. This was a bitter pill to swallow, but in my heart of hearts I knew she was right.

I quite enjoyed the applied art course but soon even that pleasure had to cease: Mother wrote to say that Father had lost his job and that there was no money to pay for my stay in Paris. I must return home. It was a sad day on which I had to part from Asya and Georgik. We all three cried when I hugged them for the last time. I thought I was leaving a big chunk of my heart in the Rue Broca.

For the last twenty years of her life Alexandra Exter lived in the Paris suburb of Fontenay-aux-Roses, where I visited her after the war. Georgik had died and she herself was ill and living in poverty and isolation. Since her death in 1949 she has come to be recognised again as a major figure in Russian art. Her work has been frequently exhibited in Europe and in the United States and is much sought after.

13

My stay in france had brought other experiences which
were memorable in their way. For two consecutive summers
I went to the Midi. When visiting me in Paris Mother had
consulted a russian *émigré* doctor about my health. The clinic
in Berlin had done wonders, but I was still rather easily tired.
The doctor examined me and found a spot on one lung, a
possible danger-sign for consumption. Nothing that lots of
sun and warmth could not cure, he assured us. And since he
owned a sanatorium on the Riviera, he would like to have me
there in his care.

So I went to Juan-les-Pins. It was not yet the fashionable,
crowded place it was to become later: there were only a few
shops and one small hotel in the village, and its superb,
mile-long sandy beach was almost empty. The only sign-
post to the future was the elegant little casino perched

above the beach: cars could be seen driving towards it in the evenings.

My sanatorium, Villa des Chrysanthèmes, was just a small-ish villa in a biggish garden, surrounded by similar villas with similar names. The gardens were all full of flowering bushes with large, orange and mauve, heavily scented blossoms. It was my first visit to the south and the magic of it took my breath away. It was marvellous, yet I didn't feel at home in it. Used to the misty light and pale grey skies of my native northern land, I found this southern landscape unreal, artificial, spectacular rather than beautiful, almost theatrical. Against the rocky backcloth of the Corniche the wide sweep of the Golfe Juan was like a vast stage under the glaring sun. At night, sitting on my balcony (mine was the only room with a balcony at the villa), after I was supposed to have gone to bed, I was awed by the immensity of the moonlit velvety sky with the multitudes of stars much brighter than I have ever seen; and the nightingales trilled in the silent gardens. A fairy-land indeed. Oh, I knew that for people who lived and worked here, it was real enough, but for me, as a spectator and outsider, it was not for living but only for dreaming in. And I was quite prepared to dream away.

In fact, my stay at the Villa des Chrysanthèmes was any-thing but a fairytale; it was incredibly dreary. Most of the patients were middle-aged Russian ladies and they bored me to tears. The youngest, who was only about six years older than I was, immediately attached herself to me. She was not herself a patient – in fact she was as strong as a horse – but she was shepherding her little girl, a puny child of six or seven. She had, she told me, been married before she was sixteen to an officer in the Russian Imperial Army; the marriage was not happy and she obviously did not miss him. She was beautiful in a classical Greek style, large, statuesque, with regular features, quite expressionless but for a permanently pouting mouth. I called her Juno. She became the bane of my life. Unfortunately the doctor assigned her and her little daughter to be my companions and their incessant chatter quite spoiled the days for me. I could neither read nor, what I liked above anything else, sit alone, in silence, weaving my dreams.

We stayed in Juan-les-Pins the whole of the summer, long after all the other visitors had gone, and in late October the doctor and his wife packed their trunks and a lorry took their furniture and luggage to a small hotel in St Maurice, in the hills above Nice. Of his 'regulars' the doctor was taking only Juno and her little daughter and me with him.

The hotel at St Maurice was owned by two Russian ladies, a countess and a baroness. The countess was engaged to a prince who drove a taxi in Nice. The Riviera was full of White Russians who had flocked there after the defeat of the White armies in the Civil War. They mostly found it hard to earn a living. Thus Juno's husband was running a chicken farm, which hardly prospered. In our hotel the countess cooked and the baroness served the meals. The baroness's husband fetched and carried, and they all shared in making beds and sweeping floors.

It was out of season and there were very few visitors in the hotel and very few patients for the doctor. But I remember the great fuss and bustle created by the arrival of a Russian grand duchess, a cousin of the Tsar, from Addis Ababa. She came to consult our doctor as no doctor in Abyssinia was able to cure her of a persistent cough. I rather liked her: small, vivacious and talkative, she accepted me as better than nothing, in the absence of any other audience. She was not a bit formal and soon chatted to me in the most natural manner. She gladly provided me with the story of her life: she had left Russia with plenty of money and jewels ('loads of them, m'dear, simply loads!') and went straight to Addis Ababa, according to her a place where there were many palaces and many servants and where one could still live in style and 'quite cheaply, m'dear'. I was sorry when she left.

By then it was mid-November and the weather turned quite nasty. When it was not raining it was blowing, and often both. Our daily walks, on which the doctor still insisted, had become unutterably boring. I suggested to Juno that we might take the tram into Nice and explore the old city or else walk along the Promenade des Anglais to the Hôtel Negresco. The latter immediately appealed to Juno, her pout even disappeared and she proposed that at the end of our walk we might go into the Negresco and sit for a while in the foyer, and even, perhaps, treat ourselves to a coffee.

The short tram ride brought us right down to the harbour, near the flower market. I would have loved to stroll around in the old part of the town but I could see that the market stalls were locked up and streets deserted. If only I had been in Nice in spring! As it was, I yielded to Juno's urging to walk on.

The Promenade des Anglais ran parallel to the shore and began very near the tram terminus. But there were in those days hardly any buildings flanking it just there, though there were ornamental street lights and seats at regular intervals. It was raining, the wind blew furiously, the sky was grey and the Negresco seemed a long way off. We huddled in our coats and scarves and marched resolutely on. For once Juno did not complain. Her enthusiasm aroused, she was unstoppable: 'Do you think we will meet interesting people in the Negresco? Beautiful, fashionable ladies, interesting, elegant men?' She needed a sharp put-down, I thought, so I said coldly that she was a romantic fool and that she was as likely to find 'interesting' people in the Negresco as to see Ivan Mazhukhin there. Ivan Mazhukhin had been the idol and heart-throb of the pre-revolutionary Russian cinema, and Juno, I knew, simply worshipped him. Now she was pouting again.

The road did not seem to get any shorter and it was quite deserted but for a dark speck in the distance. This grew slowly and revealed itself as a human figure, a man, striding towards us. While we had been slowed down by the wind, he was fairly whipped forward by it, the skirts of his coat and the ends of his scarf flapping about him. At one moment his hat was almost blown away and he raised both his hands to ram it hard on the back of his head. Now he was beside us and his features could be clearly seen. He did not look at us, staring before him with concentrated – what was it, fury, frustration or simply the effort of fighting the wind? I could not tell, but I could, we both could, tell who the man was. It was Ivan Mazhukhin.

My second visit to Juan-les-Pins, in the following summer, was very different from the first. I brought company with me and found more there. My two companions were two sisters whom I had met the previous winter in Paris: Sarah, the elder, studious, sedate and already promised to a young man approved by her parents; and Kiki, empty-headed, flirtatious and completely out of control. Sarah was good-looking in her quiet way, but Kiki was really pretty, small and slim and dressed in every detail like a 'flapper'. The two sisters were incompatible and Sarah had very wisely refused to look after Kiki. In Paris, before our departure, her mother had implored me, too, to keep an eye on Kiki, but this proved beyond my power.

I had hoped for my dear room with balcony but found on arrival that that room was occupied by a young man from Moscow and that we three girls were to share a large room on the ground floor. I found other changes in Juan-les-Pins; a luxury hotel was being built overlooking the beach, and the beach itself was much fuller than the year before – brightly coloured sun umbrellas were everywhere. Under one of these could be found, any time of the day, reading or dozing, the young man who had usurped my room with the balcony. He was Igor Stanislavsky, son of the famous actor-director of the Moscow Art Theatre. According to our doctor, he was very seriously ill with consumption and had to have as much rest as possible. He was a tall, lanky and pale youth with a vague expression and a sweet smile; I found him easy to talk to and to make friends with. He complained that he was too much cosseted by the doctor, restricted to his sun umbrella by day and tucked in not later than nine o'clock in the evening. He hated being ill. We had endless talks under the umbrella about his life and we agreed that his health would never improve in these circumstances; he was fretting and fuming and that was surely bad for him. We decided to change all that. No sooner had the doctor said goodnight to Igor and closed the door than I climbed up from the garden on to the balcony (I was no acrobat but there was a convenient ledge) and helped Igor to dress again. Then we installed ourselves on the balcony and whispered and sipped Cinzano, which I had brought with me, to our hearts' content. Sometimes we did more: Igor put on evening clothes, I helped him down the balcony pillar to the garden path and we made for the casino.

The glittering world of the casino had been revealed to me by Kiki. She had lost no time in making conquests and was in fact submerged in a crowd of young people – the *jeunesse dorée* of Juan-les-Pins. She spent most of her evenings at the casino, dancing to a small orchestra in the elegant ballroom that adjoined the gaming-rooms. Kiki's pals were mostly summer visitors, but she had also made friends with some local French youths. The undisputed leader of these was Jacques, the young son of a French count and an American mother, who lived in a real château above the Corniche; he was masterful, good-looking and a brilliant dancer. It was Kiki's dream to dance with him. When the charleston reached us, and a group of vaudeville girls danced it on the stage of our casino, the spectators were electrified. The exuberance, the vitality of it! Everybody was made to learn it, but Jacques was the first to master it and he did it so well that he was adopted by '*les girls*' to perform with them on stage. Charleston went to our heads; I had never seen such frenzy. Leaving Igor at a table with a drink, I too joined the rest of them on the dance floor, chanting, clapping, rocking, swinging legs and knocking knees. To my surprise I was singled out by Jacques. He had never noticed me before and even now he didn't actually notice me, he just annexed me. Together we shone on the dance floor. Charleston was a real American dance revolution and it swept Europe. I had had some inkling of the freedom of the American style before – when I had danced with the young physicist from Princeton in Berlin – but this was freer still.

The charleston made everything American immensely popular on the Riviera. One morning, on the beach, Kiki saw an American college boy in wide trousers and brightly patterned pullover; he was sitting on the sand, playing 'Yes, sir, that's my baby . . .' on a portable gramophone; Kiki at once fell in love with him.

But summer was coming to an end. Sarah and a tearful Kiki went back to Paris; Jacques was to escort his Mama to Biarritz. I was pronounced by the doctor to be quite recovered and was to leave soon. But before I left I had an unforgettable day. Igor's mother, the actress Lilina, arrived from Moscow. She was staying at our villa for a week and she invited me to take tea with her. The tea table was laid in the garden under some trees which looked like young Russian birches. Lilina, a frail and gentle lady, all lace and shawls, was very beautiful and gracious. I felt as if I was on the stage of the Moscow Art Theatre, in one of Stanislavsky's productions of a Chekhov play. She thanked me for being so kind to Igor, for taking such care of him. I had never felt more guilty; had I perhaps made him more ill than he already was, even hastened his death? I had acted as I did because both he and I felt that boredom was killing him, but were we right to deceive the doctor, and now his mother? That question nagged at me for many years.

Finally, sometime in the 1960s or 70s, on the occasion of an exhibition of Stanislavsky's work in London, I asked the organiser of the exhibition whether, when in Moscow, he had met Stanislavsky's son Igor. Was he well? 'Yes indeed,' said the man, 'he was very helpful and energetic.' I was really relieved.

14

BACK IN BERLIN I found many changes at home. The government in Moscow had put an end to the relative tolerance hitherto enjoyed by *émigré* Mensheviks, and all the Mensheviks employed abroad by the Soviet Foreign Trade Ministry had lost their jobs. Father had occupied quite a prominent position and drawn a good salary. Now he was working for much less pay as an accountant for a private firm.

My brother Danya had graduated from the technological university and moved to the factory district of Wedding, where he lived in digs near his work and where he soon married a local girl. My parents had also moved, from the spacious flat in quiet, leafy Grünewald to a smaller flat in the middle of town. Still, Mother continued to entertain lavishly. It was rare for us to sit down to dinner by ourselves; usually there were four or five or even six guests. It was nothing new for Mother to manage on little money, and her dinners were still excellent.

With the change of flat there seemed also to have occurred a great change in the composition of our dinner parties. There were fewer Mensheviks. Almost permanent guests were three Polish socialists and the Menshevik Yury Petrovich Denike. I soon discovered that these four were in fact a team, working unofficially for Maxim Litvinov, the Deputy Commissar for Foreign Affairs of the Soviet Union – a small private think-tank that read, digested, analysed and summarised for him the whole international political scene.

The talk at the dinner table in our new flat was exclusively political and often it was above my head. The only light relief came from Yury Petrovich, who liked to joke with me. Sometimes after dinner we would push odd chairs and small tables out of the way, he and I, and he would teach me old dances. Our favourite was the *machisse*. The tall, lanky and awkward Denike would sing, or rather croak the words, while his long legs jerked out in all directions like a puppet's: *'C'est la dance espagnole . . . c'est le machisse!'* (And then the same in Russian.)

A new visitor, new to me at least, was Frederic Voigt, the Berlin correspondent of the *Manchester Guardian*. He was first brought to see us by, I believe, Denike. Hearing that he lived only a few houses away down our street, Mother at once extended a standing invitation. It was she explained, a Russian custom to drop in on friends any time that one saw a light in the window. Voigt certainly liked that custom and often dropped in, for dinner or after.

Voigt belonged to that brand of high-powered, highly individualistic foreign correspondents who descended on Central Europe in the late 1920s. During his years in Berlin he not only became an expert on German politics but acquired a deep understanding of the Soviet regime. All this was to find expression, years later, in a remarkable book entitled *Unto Caesar* (Constable, 1938). There he argued that Communism and German National Socialism were both forms of secularised millenarianism – an idea which now is something of a commonplace, but which at the time was startlingly new. No doubt it was Voigt's professional interests that drew him to the 'Litvinov' team and to our dinner table. But he also made great friends with Father, whom in later days he described as one of the most intelligent men he ever met.

I myself knew very little, at that time, about Father's political views. I sometimes wondered why it was that he took no part in the activities of the *émigré* Mensheviks. I know now that his views on Russian affairs differed widely from the views held by Mother and by most of our guests. He had, I think, become convinced that there was no future for democratic socialism in Russia, that the defeat of the Mensheviks was irreversible, and that their activities at home and abroad were futile. Among the Mensheviks he kept his views to himself, but to Voigt – to whom he usually spoke in English – he revealed them readily enough. And they talked of much else beside politics, as they sat a little apart at the end of the dinner. Father loved England and all things English, in particular literature. Voigt was widely read (his special subject at university had been Anglo-Saxon) and Father found in him a kindred spirit.

When I arrived from Paris, Voigt was already firmly established as one of our 'regulars'. I was not that interested in the
exclusively political talk that circulated round the table, so I
naturally inclined to listen in on the talks between Father and
Voigt. When I said that I was sorry that my English was so
poor, Voigt offered to teach me. I was delighted and so was
Father. So for a time I went over to Voigt's flat once or twice
a week for lessons.

Voigt's study, where we were to have the lessons, was an
enormous room, but tables, shelves, chairs and even floor
were spilling over with papers and books. There were several
very good pictures on the walls and on the highest of the
bookshelves sat a live owl! I was so fascinated by the curious
objects in the room and had so many questions to ask that
our hour usually passed only too quickly. I found that apart
from literature Voigt was also interested in the arts: he owned
several Expressionist paintings, particularly by Emil Nolde,
and a huge collection of records. After my time with
Alexandra Exter I was at home in the world of painting but
not in music: neither of my parents was musical and there
was no music in the house. Voigt's records were a delight and
he seemed to enjoy my enthusiasm. In fact he was very happy
to be my guide and mentor in all the arts and I could not have
found a better one. And not only a mentor but a true friend
and often a guardian angel.

I made another excursion into the world of music: I became
a pupil of the leading singing teacher in Berlin. It came about
in the following way: Nina, one of my friends from the
Russian school, often came to spend the evening with me

and these evenings often ended with me singing Russian folk songs. Nina liked nothing better than to curl up on my bed and listen to me. I had always loved Russian songs and knew a great many of them, so I did not need much urging. One evening Nina brought a young man with her, who, unknown to me, was studying operatic singing with the foremost *bel canto* teacher in Berlin. When Nina asked me to sing, I sang, unembarrassed as ever, and was surprised when the young man urged me to come with him to see his teacher: 'You have a voice to be trained and he will train it!' So, before I had the time to think it out seriously, I was taken to the famous man (his pupils included Richard Tauber and many other stars). He had studied *bel canto* in Italy, but found that he was unemployable in opera: he was very short, barrel-chested, with a bull head and a bit of a hunchback. There was really only one part for him in all opera – in *Pagliacci* – and no-one could build a career on one part. So he became a teacher and settled in Berlin. When he was sitting at the piano, his physical disadvantages did not show and his voice was powerful and very expressive.

The maestro greeted me courteously, asked me to sing to him and, to my surprise, didn't reject me out of hand. In fact, he offered to take me as a pupil for three years; after that, he said, I would never be out of work as an opera singer. I was staggered, but when I said that I had no money (his fees, I knew, were exorbitant), he waved it aside; he would train me for nothing, against fifty per cent of all my future earnings, so sure was he of my success! I was plunged into a dream, and still in a dream I said yes. At first I worked for him with great enthusiasm, doing endless breathing exercises before the open window and singing endless scales, to the despair of my family. I was overjoyed when after only a few weeks I was allowed to sing an Italian song (I think it was by Pergolesi); I was already dreaming of becoming a *diva*, of travelling the world from one opera house to another. But it was not to be. After about three months I found my teacher's arm circling my waist rather intimately when we sat side by side at the piano, and I realised with a shock how naive I had been.

Fortunately I had no time to brood; Mother needed me in her new enterprise. Even before I returned from Paris, Father's diminished earnings had made her look around for ways to supplement them. It was not an easy time: Berlin, the whole of Germany, was in financial straits. Mother fell back on a source of income that she had found rewarding before, back in Russia, particularly in Siberian exile – dressmaking. 'Be there war, revolution, or just inflation, women will still want clothes,' she said. She promptly set up a dressmaking and alterations service in our flat, putting it about that her daughter, who had been trained as a dress designer in Paris, would shortly be joining her. She was quite undeterred by her own lack of chic or by my complete lack of experience. She firmly believed that a strong will and determination would overcome all obstacles. All that was needed, to begin with, was a sewing-machine, a full-length mirror and a few fashion magazines.

I was pitchforked into this crazy enterprise as soon as I arrived, and I realised that I would either sink or learn to swim quickly. I did my best: made sketches of 'modish' dresses and designer hats. The hats were actually made by a Russian *émigré* lady who had set herself up as a *modiste* in our neighbourhood. I remember bringing her some of my designs and helping her to choose some felts for them. She was a middle-aged, stout body with the manners of a society lady, but her language was earthy. Diving into a huge carton containing felts of all shades and sizes, she triumphantly emerged with one in her hand: 'This is it,' she crooned, 'such a rich cow dung!'

Mother's 'salon' did quite well, but not well enough for her liking. So she next found a small shop in a fashionable square and promptly opened a 'model house'. The shop had previously been a cobbler's and the rent was low, but we poshed it up inside. Our full-length mirror was installed behind full-length satin curtains which formed a cubicle; and several chairs, bought cheaply at an auction and painted lacquer red by me, stood around in the shop. Behind the shop was the workroom with a long deal table, on which the sewing-machine had pride of place. Mother engaged a cutter-fitter, who had previously worked in a real fashion house, and an embroidery woman, a small hunchback, who did wonders with her fine, sensitive hands. And because the cutter was, in technical terms, a master cutter and had the right to take on aspiring seamstresses, we also had two or three apprentices in the workroom.

Having set up the business, Mother considered that she had provided for me; I was, after all, nearly twenty. It did not occur to her that there was no capital to make the business viable. Next she announced that she was leaving for Russia. I was completely stunned, and so was Father. Swearing us to secrecy, Mother explained that the Menshevik Delegation in Exile had been from time to time sending couriers to keep contact with Mensheviks in Russia. Now, in 1927, it was important to send somebody with experience and authority. Such journeys were, of course, not without danger: one travelled with false documents, crossed the border illegally and, once inside the country, dodged the secret police as best one could. If all went well, one was expected to return after six weeks, and Mother assured us that she was confident she would return to us after that time.

As it turned out, she found so much to see and so much to do that she stayed on and on, travelling all over the country. She was arrested after six months and imprisoned without trial. We never saw her again.

15

Within a year of Mother's departure I had to wind up my model house. On the face of it, it was a great success, and my order books were full to overflowing. But rent and weekly wages had to be paid on the dot while customers paid their bills after long delays or not at all.

Father came every evening after work to look over my account book, and together we tried to figure out what to do. Then Father helped me to shut the shop and we walked home, there to worry some more. For both of us this worry about the shop masked a greater worry – about Mother. We did not talk about her – we talked endlessly about the wretched shop. But there was no remedy: I had to close down.

I was lucky enough to find a small secretarial job, which paid enough to keep me afloat. But Father's employment in

Berlin was precarious, and when he was offered a more secure appointment in Danzig, I persuaded him to take it. It was a sad parting.

Danya was still working in distant Wedding, and I seldom saw him. I saw little, either, of Mother's Menshevik friends, whom I rather blamed for her fate. Yet they had for so long been my extended family that I missed them. I felt very alone. But in the end I did make some friends among German students and artists, and sometimes went to their evening gatherings. I liked to be liked, and I felt that they liked me; they even gave me an affectionate nickname: *sibirisches Pferdchen* (Siberian pony). My red mane was still my hallmark.

It was at one of those evening parties that I first met Raoul Hausmann. He was a stocky man, with a short neck on top of broad shoulders, and he was not handsome. Nor did I like his monocle, or the exaggerated cut of his clothes; in fact, I found something showy and peacocky about him. Yet the man had presence, he was a good talker, he held the room captive. I sat back in a corner and was trying to sort out my impressions when, just as Hausmann and his wife were leaving, he came up to me and made a most unexpected suggestion: they were going on holiday in a few days' time – would I care to join them? It seemed a wonderful offer, and it could not have come at a better time. I needed a holiday, and I had no ties in Berlin. So a few days later I went off with the Hausmanns to Kampen, on the Frisian island of Sylt.

When I so light-heartedly agreed to go with the Hausmanns I did not expect to be precipitated into a *ménage à trois*. I did not even understand that Raoul wanted me for a lover – after all, he was double my age. And at first I was embarrassed and uneasy. But his wife, Heta, was more than welcoming. She was a gentle, quiet woman whose identification with her husband was such that what he wanted, she wanted. At that moment he wanted me, and so she did everything to make me stay. Her refrain, re-echoed down the years was: 'He *needs* you. . .'

No doubt I was flattered. After all he was a well-known artist, a celebrity in his youth. He was still a powerful, even charismatic personality, half-genius and half-mad. But this is not an unusual mix in an artist and there was no doubt that he was a versatile and original artist: painter, writer, dancer, photographer. The artist in him fascinated me. And if he also 'needed' me (as what – muse, audience or sparring partner?) well then – so be it. I stayed on and even developed a kind of commitment, as if I had entered a contract, every bit as binding as a marriage contract. In the event I stayed for almost seven years.

By the time I met him, Raoul Hausmann had actually left most of his artistic activities behind, concentrating almost exclusively on photography. But he often talked about his past and he was a good talker, so that I could piece together his early life. He was born in Vienna, of Czech parents (though there seemed to have been some French and some Jewish blood in them). He learnt painting from his father, who was a conventional painter and even after the family had moved to Germany, father and son worked together, sometimes on murals. There was hardly anything left of this early work, except for some self-portraits which are certainly very fine. By the time I knew him he had quite given up painting and I never saw him hold a paint brush. That he had not lost his painting skills I discovered quite by chance, when I rescued from the wastepaper basket a crumpled pastel (of me reading), a masterly study of red hair cascading over a much foreshortened face. It is lovely and I still own it.

His work and his life changed completely when he joined the Berlin group of Dadaists. This was undoubtedly the high point of his artistic career. Discounting some rivalries and personal prejudices, I can see, in the light of later knowledge, that his account of the development of Dadaism was on the whole a balanced one. He had called himself Dadasoph from the first and it seems to me that he certainly understood the aims and the inner logic of Dadaism better than most of the others. Dada claimed to be anti-ideology, in fact anti-strait-jacket of any kind – political, moral or aesthetic.

Above all, of course, Dada was anti-art, in every conventional sense of the word. Its main weapon was ridicule; by exaggeration and buffoonery everything was reduced to absurdity, that is to Dada, the Ultimate Absurd. All this was familiar to me from Russian Futurism: the iconoclasm, the urge to destroy everything, the desire to shock, also the vanity, the narcissism and self-advertisement. But Dada was perhaps even more extreme. Hausmann wrote: 'We put aside the folly of good taste,' and 'Whoever eats of Dada without being dada, dies of it. Dada owes it to itself to remain indigestible.'

Such a total rejection of a society that has run itself into a rut is a familiar and sometimes healthy phenomenon. Unfortunately, both in Russia and in Germany many of these uncompromising iconoclasts fell into the trap of Communism, which turned out to be even more restrictive and retrograde than the bourgeois society they rebelled against. At least Hausmann – unlike, for instance, John

Heartfield and his brother Wieland Herzfelde, Georg Grosz, Franz Jung – never toyed with Communism.

Dada was violent but short-lived. Already in 1920/21 Hausmann wrote, 'Dada is dead.' When I knew him he had withdrawn from most of his former activities and was living a very quiet life, with Heta, in a comfortable flat in Berlin. He rarely went out, but he did keep in touch with some of his former friends.

Of those friends I liked Salomo Friedlaender (Mynona) best. A professional philosopher, he wrote short stories in his spare time. They appealed to me greatly and I still possess a slim volume of them. The best, I think, is the story called 'The Gentle Giant'. The giant is loving and full of goodwill towards all living creatures, but he is so big and so heavy that with every step he takes he crushes hundreds of them to death. He is inconsolable; he sits and cries – but what can he do? To me this seemed a portrait of Mynona himself. I have never met a kinder, more considerate person.

The only regular visitors to the flat were Johannes Baader and Kurt Schwitters. But Baader now lived in Hamburg and Schwitters in Hanover, so that even these were infrequent guests. I always looked forward to Baader's visits: tall and handsome, with perfect manners, he was immensely likeable. Hausmann was very fond of him and often talked about him. He told me of his beginnings: he had been a talented and successful architect, married, with children, when – and this from Baader's own account – he was struck dead by an overhead electric bulb at the entrance to the railway station in Leipzig. There was a wide flight of stairs leading down to the street and he was just stepping out of the doorway when it happened. Death was instantaneous, Baader said: 'One moment I was alive and the next I was dead. But nothing changed; though dead I moved down the stairs with the rest of the crowd, only now I perceived that some of the others were dead too.'

When Hausmann first met him, Baader had already stopped work as an architect; it was his wife who kept the family going, writing tracts for the feminist movement, running a crèche for infants. It was quite bizarre, said Hausmann: there she was at her desk, totally absorbed in writing or typing, while the infants propelled themselves, each sitting on his or her chamber pot, round and round the room, unheeded. Bills piled up and there was little money but Baader took no notice. However, when the landlord threatened eviction, he suddenly acted. He went to the public library and consulted some legal tomes, from which he learnt, or thought he learnt, that if a painter painted frescoes all over a wall, that wall became his property. What applied to a painter should apply to a poet, he reasoned, so he promptly wrote poetry all over the walls of the house. In the end they had to move out, but it had earned them a respite while the case was being argued.

It was about this time that Hausmann met Baader and he immediately realised two things: that Baader was genuinely insane and that he had imagination and talent. Who could be better than a madman to preside over Dada? He straightaway pronounced Baader Ober-Dada (Head Dada) and staged several public appearances with him. Together they practised what Hausmann called 'psycho-analytical cacophony': simultaneous reading of incoherent passages from some masterpiece of world literature – rather like the famous race between a sewing-machine and a typewriter, staged by the Dadaists Grosz and Mehring. On one occasion, an empty shop was rented for a few days and while Hausmann and Heartfield sold tickets at the door, behind a curtain, in an inner room, the bearded Baader was enthroned on a red plush sofa – stark naked. There was nothing else to see. The curious citizens who had paid for their tickets were puzzled but also indignant, rushing to get their money back and finding the birds flown.

I think that Hausmann manipulated Baader, which was easy enough because Baader did not always see the distinction between the normal and the abnormal. But he was no fool; in fact he was every bit as intelligent as Hausmann and quite capable of acting on his own, sometimes to Hausmann's annoyance. Some of his pranks, as Hausmann called them, were quite risky. For instance, during the war he threw Dada anti-war pamphlets from the public gallery in the Reichstag in Berlin. Later he distributed his own pamphlet *Grüne Leiche* (green corpse) in the National Assembly in Weimar. He also demanded the replacement of the government by Dada and announced the imminent coming of Ober-Dada on a white horse as the Supreme Judge in the Last Judgement. It is a wonder that he was not seized and imprisoned then and there. Somewhat later he was in fact tried, with Grosz, Heartfield and Schlichter (not Hausmann, but only because he was of Czech nationality) for slandering the name of the German army.

Baader's mental illness was cyclical and between bouts he was quite in control and able to work. In Hamburg, he was employed as a reporter by the *Hamburger Fremdenblatt*. But when he felt his illness coming on, he packed his suitcase, took a typewriter and went to the mental clinic or hospital of his choice (he said he liked to go to the mountains in winter and the seaside in summer), rang the bell, said that he came as a patient and asked to be shown to a room where he could type out his case history. And this, apparently, was always quite accurate.

When Baader came to Berlin, he always visited Raoul. I took to him greatly. He was easy to talk to and he himself talked easily and, on the whole, quite rationally. Only some-times did I glimpse the otherness of his mind. Thus once he said that on his way to see us he couldn't make his way through the crowds in Steglitz. 'Why?' I asked, 'what crowds?' He looked at me somewhat impatiently: 'There are always crowds in Steglitz,' he said, 'crowds of dead people. They choke the streets so that one can hardly move.' Often his madness was spiced with slyness. Thus, on the occasion of a dairy festival in Hamburg he wrote an article for his paper entitled 'The Milky Way'. He explained to us that his editor had accepted the article as a pleasant joke while he had meant it not as a joke at all but as a serious treatise on the Milky Way and the Cosmos (everything Baader wrote was always con-cerned with the Cosmos). Another time he told us how he went to a convention of 'Christs'. At that time there were so many men in Germany claiming to be messiahs – and some had numerous followers – that they agreed to come together in Thuringia to establish once and for all which of them was the real one. Baader was asked by his editor to report on this evening, and so he got Lufthansa to fly him to the venue, landing right amidst them. Baader was extremely pleased with himself and the dramatic effect he produced: 'There was this large meadow and there they all were, standing in a wide circle, with their "apostles" around them, and there was I, coming in majesty down from heaven: a Christ of Christs!'

Whenever we met Baader in the café in Hamburg he showed us his latest book of drawings. They were mainly linear abstracts, which betrayed his original training as an architect but showed also great imagination and complexity. Some of them were delicately coloured and all had great beauty of line and composition. Vaguely they all related to Baader's preoccupation with the Cosmos, though their meaning remained obscure to me. He had apparently filled several heavy albums with these drawings; I myself saw two volumes.

Kurt Schwitters was a very different man from Baader. Whereas Baader looked rather romantic, Schwitters was depressingly commonplace. He looked what indeed he was – a minor civil servant, not the dapper but rather the drab kind. He was employed by the Hanover town council for which he designed letterheads, official announcements and the like. He always wore a dark office-type suit and when he came to Berlin, he stayed – he said for reasons of economy – in dingy little hotels where one paid by the hour. Yet he was a true artist and highly imaginative. His collages have rightly become famous. Strictly speaking he never belonged to the Dadaists (he called his art Merz), but he had often gone on tours of exhibitions with Hausmann. There was a feeling of friendly rivalry between the two men. They vied with each other in the composition of sound poems ('optophonetic' or 'phonetic' poems), at which Hausmann excelled, and in making collages, at which Schwitters excelled.

I had little rapport with Schwitters and was surprised when

he invited me to go with him to the *Katakombe* cabaret. I was to collect Schwitters from the hotel in the early evening. I found the dingy hotel in a dingy street and his room was no better. He was in bed, having rested, he explained, after an exhausting day in town. However, he put on a clean shirt and was soon his usual correct self. Downstairs he paid his bill (for two hours, I remember), as he planned to take a night train home. When we left the hotel, he steered me firmly into the middle of the thoroughfare, which a few days' rotten weather had left full of slush and dirt. Walking slowly and bent low, Schwitters prodded the dirt with his foot, pouncing on anything bright and glittering that came to light: discarded cigar bands, bits of bright wrapping paper, green or red ticket stumps, or metal of any kind – all were stuffed into the pockets of his suit, where he also kept some loose sweets. He offered me some of those sweets, but I was not tempted. The whole scene reminded me vividly of one of the short stories by Mynona, where the street-sweeper picks prunes out of the horse dung that he is sweeping up and pops them into his mouth with obvious enjoyment. A passing lady is almost sick at the sight, but the street-sweeper reproves her; why waste what is full of goodness and sustaining life? The bright bits that Schwitters was picking up were also full of goodness, because they were giving life and substance to his collages.

When we arrived at the *Katakombe*, I saw in the programme the reason for our being there: in the second half there was an item called *Anna Blume* or *Love through the Ages. Anna Blume* was the title of one of Schwitters's poems. I had read some of his poems and liked them very much. Most of the programme consisted of political satire and was, as always in the *Katakombe*, sharp and witty. But the piece we had come to watch turned out to be a poorly scripted and badly acted series of sketches of love through the ages, *Anna Blume* typifying our own time. And the two young players ridiculed and burlesqued Schwitters's fine poem out of existence. I was boiling with indignation, but he remained calm and said nothing. As we were drifting out of the theatre with other spectators, somebody must have recognised him; there was a stir, one of the actors rushed after us and we were invited to join the company for a late supper on the stage. When we accepted and turned back we found that trestle tables were being moved on to the stage and we were being, somewhat apologetically, welcomed by the director. What did we think of the show? 'Fine, fine,' Schwitters was not giving anything away. But once the supper was over somebody suggested that he read his poem, and this he did, without any fuss. I knew him for a fine poet and I knew that he read his poems beautifully, but somehow this setting, the stage, the company of professional actors – it all heightened the occasion.

Anna, du bist von vorne wie von hinten – Anna.
Anna, du bist von vorne wie von hinten – schön!
(Anna, you are from the front and from the back – Anna.
Anna, you are from the front and from the back –
    beautiful!)

There was complete silence for a moment and then the two young players came stumbling forward and stood shamefaced before Schwitters. What could they say . . . so clumsy, so inept . . . they were truly sorry!

Another visitor to our flat – an unforgettable one – was Dovzhenko. He had always been my favourite among

Russian film-makers. I resented the crude propaganda in Eisenstein's films but I was prepared to forgive the propaganda in Dovzhenko's work because I considered him politically naive. I loved his films for the sheer poetry in them. His film *Earth* sang and glowed with beauty.

It was Hans Richter, the German avant-garde filmmaker, who brought Dovzhenko to us, because Richter spoke no Russian and Dovzhenko no German and I was asked to interpret. Dovzhenko was a typical Ukrainian, slow of speech and gesture, but he was obviously brimful of ideas and plans for future work. He seemed completely immersed in his visions and had no time for smalltalk. Richter wanted to know whether he had started experimenting with sound! Oh, indeed he had, it opened such a field of possibilities! But he would not use sound simply as an extension of acting; he wanted to use it as an independent element. 'Imagine a wide, wide river in Siberia in early spring; the ice has begun to break up and it is no longer possible to cross it on foot; there is a wedding to be celebrated in the village on one side of the river, but the priest has to come from a village on the other side: the bride in her white dress, the bridegroom in his dark suit and the whole congregation has come down to the river's edge, while the priest stands on the far shore, unable to join them; he decides to conduct the service nevertheless; the river is very wide and the black figure of the priest, his arms outstretched, seems smaller than life, but his deep voice is powerful and it floats slowly and fully over the creaking, breaking ice floes. For a while the service proceeds smoothly, the responses of the bridal pair and the wedding guests are feeble murmurings against the full-throated intonations of the priest. But then there is a violent disruption: the priest is attacked and overpowered by wolves and while he dies in full view of his shocked parishioners, the last sounds of his voice, a benediction, are still floating solemnly across the river . . .' I was overwhelmed by the picture he had drawn so vividly, and found it very difficult to convey, in my translation, its full impact. It helped that I had known Siberian rivers in spring in my childhood and still felt the awe and the fear of them in my bones.

But, on the whole, visitors were rare in the Hausmann household. Most evenings we spent at home, usually listening to jazz records, of which Raoul had many. Occasionally Hausmann would dance; sometimes to a jazz record and sometimes altogether without music. He usually danced dressed in a pair of old summer trousers with wide bottoms, barefoot and with torso bare. And though his legs hardly moved, his arms, chest and face were in constant movement, and muscular tension could be felt from his toes to the top of his head. In his article on the death of Dada, written around 1920, when he was already disillusioned with the movement and estranged from most of his former associates, he wrote: '. . . I seek a new direction, prescribed by the organisation of my body'. I think that new direction inspired most of his post-Dadaist work. Certainly it led him to elaborate his extraordinary dances – they were indeed dictated by an inner bodily law to the exclusion of conscious mind. To me he explained that in dancing he first destroyed and then built up anew the space around him; it was a battle between body and space, body imprisoned in space freeing itself. But whatever the theory behind it, his dancing was strikingly original and compelling.

Sometimes he danced only with his face. Dressed in the same manner he would sit down under a strong light and move only his face and the muscles of his neck, the rest of his body remaining motionless. It was amazing how much variety he achieved in this self-restricting way. It was so absorbing to watch that it was always something of a shock when the record ended and he stopped. One marvelled that he could sustain a never boring, never repetitive effort for so long.

On other evenings Hausmann would recite some of his *Laut-Gedichte* (tone poems), which consisted of single sounds projected into space at different degrees of volume, speed and level of voice, the mouth sometimes seemingly catching them from the air and at other times almost spitting them out. The total effect was of a vocal eruption without words but with a compelling inner force and cohesion. It was no cacophony, rather a chant in an unknown language and an unknown musical notation. In print these rows of letters – OFFEAHBDC etc. – look meaningless but when intoned they came to life, were full of passion, of anguish. But I liked it best when he improvised on vowels only: O a o a o a O A Eeeee . . .

It was photography that now preoccupied him, one might say obsessed him. Camera at the ready and monocle firmly in place (he told me that his other eye was completely blind and the good eye was much more serviceable with a monocle than with spectacles), he would, like a hunter, stalk his prey. And like a hunter, he was so silent, so self-effacing that often one did not know he was near, until the click betrayed him. When in town he sometimes photographed out of doors – cobbled streets, rain in the dusk and so on, but rarely; mostly he found his subjects indoors and mostly they were studies of faces, of heads, of shoulders – awake, asleep, in repose, often reading, always unaware of being photographed. In the country the choice was wider, though he looked rather for the detail, the minutiae than for the wide views. He looked for roadside plants, weeds, particularly early in the year, when flat rosettes of leaves form on the ground or small shoots of stems appear like miniature soldiers on parade. And when photographing the sea, it was not the foaming, mountainous waves but rather the shallow waters running over the pebbly sand that appealed to him. His main subject however was the nude. He would dodge and circle and wait, and only 'pounce' when the time was right.

He never staged his subjects, never arranged the poses, either indoors or outdoors. And he never retouched the photos afterwards, though he always cut them before print-ing. I would call him an honest photographer – no tricks, no subterfuges. When I look at his photos of nudes, as for instance in the book *Formes nues*,* I am struck by the fact that compared to those by other photographers in this volume, his are completely unselfconscious and therefore unembarrassing. To him nudes were no different from sand, pebbles or plants – what mattered was texture and form, objects in space and light. To me he never pointed out how original this was, but when, many years later, I met László Moholy-Nagy, himself a pioneer of modern photography, he said to me: 'Raoul has shown us all the way – he was the first.'

* Published in 1935 by FORME, Editions d'Art graphique et photo-graphique; edited by Albert Mentzel and Albert Roux.

How Raoul would have loved to hear that himself! For the last ten years in Germany, and during the thirty years that he later spent in France, he lived in comparative obscurity. It was only after his death in 1971 that his achievement came to be at all widely appreciated. Now his work is much exhibited, studied and written about.

16

In each of the years that I lived with the Hausmanns we spent a long summer by the sea, either at Kampen or at Jershöft, a village in east Pomerania on the Baltic.

Nowadays, I understand, Sylt is more crowded than Blackpool. But in those days it was a hideout for artists and writers, and Kampen, with its little pub, was still just a village. There was an incredibly long, sandy beach and, beyond it, mountainous dunes stretching far to the north, almost to Denmark. We lived in a converted village smithy which belonged to friends of the Hausmanns. Every morning we walked the length of that splendid beach to the far dunes, where we had chosen a particular crater as our own. It was an unwritten law of the local artistic fraternity that each family, couple or group of friends who wanted to sunbathe in the nude should keep to their spot in the dunes. Nudism *en masse*, which was sweeping Germany at that time, was quite a different thing. The Kampen lot liked their privacy and guarded it jealously.

It was my first experience of nudism, but I had no difficulty with it. In Russia, in the country, it was customary to bathe in rivers in the nude; and in the communal baths in Moscow I had seen hundreds of naked bodies. Later, in Paris, I had often drawn nude models, male and female. I was quite comfortable with being nude myself and with seeing others in the nude.

I loved Sylt. The long breakers of the North Sea with their foamy fringes, the dunes with their yellow-white sand – it was a landscape on a grand scale. My other experience of the sea had been on the Côte d'Azur, and bathing in the North Sea was far more exhilarating than that. What joy there was in running again and again to meet the giant waves, and spluttering and choking on salt water, and afterwards drying out on the warm sand of the dunes!

Compared with Sylt, Jershöft was rather tame, but it too had its attractions. It was a small fishing village where we rented rooms in peasant houses. In August, when there were a few families of holiday-makers, horse-drawn carts occasionally appeared, laden with vegetables, meat and groceries. The rest of the time the few long-term visitors had to survive on the fish in season and on the bread, potatoes, fat pork and chickens that the local peasants sold them. But in autumn edible fungi were plentiful in the forests, and the hedges were full of blackberries. The many happy hours that we spent gathering both the fungi and the berries more than made up for the monotony of the diet, and the evening meal of fungi fried with onions and cured pork, followed by berries in thick cream, seemed a feast.

And the dunes beyond the village, though less spectacular than on Sylt, were even more deserted. As usual we chose one particular crater as our own. There we were alone with the sea, the sun, the sand.

Each time we returned to Berlin from our holiday the political climate looked more menacing. The rise of Nazism was terrifying. From the windows of our corner house we could watch column after column of uniformed Nazis marching past – first the young men, then the young women, then the children – shouting anti-Semitic slogans. The sound made us shudder. What was happening to the country? To my parents' generation Germany was one of the most highly educated and civilised countries in Europe; German workers were among the most decent and enlightened. Much of this was still true. But inflation and mass unemployment had brought these hordes on to the streets of Berlin. The future was dark.

In 1933 we decided to take our holiday abroad. In April we left Germany for the Balearic island of Ibiza. We thought we were going simply for a long summer holiday and never imagined that we would not return.

In those days Ibiza was still untouched by mass tourism, and we at once fell in love with it. Sunwashed and sun-bleached to a golden white on its plains, rugged and dark where the sea broke into its coves, like a handkerchief edged with black lace flung upon the dark blue sea, it was beautiful beyond belief. The vegetation was rather scanty – mainly vines and olives, fig-trees and prickly pears, with here and there a few tall spikes of aloe; but there were also apricot trees, and when these were in bloom a pink haze settled over the land. That was pure magic.

But Ibiza's greatest glory lies in the peasant houses dotted over the landscape. In the purity of its lines and the perfect balance of its masses the Ibizenc *finca* is an architectural miracle. Several perfect hollow cubes are placed, in a variety of ways, so that they form one or two storeys. There are many variations on this basic cube-theme. Sometimes two cubes are placed end to end to form a long house. Sometimes a double cube – one cube on top of another – is placed alongside a single cube, so that the flat roof of the single cube serves as an open veranda. Always a wall is left protruding from an outer corner of a cube to form a patio. The roofs are always flat; often they serve as cisterns for rainwater, for wells are rare. The whole structure, walls and roofs, is whitewashed and blindingly bright in the strong southern light. Sometimes the stark geometrical lines are relieved by small alcoves in the walls, or by wooden gates, or by railings on the verandas. The walls are very thick and the windows very small, to keep the house cool in summer. Often there are no panes on the windows.

It is a building technique that allows for growth. The first cube or two cubes form a house large enough for a young married couple; usually it is built by the young man himself, with the help of relatives or neighbours. But as the family grows, so the house grows with it, as more and more cubes are added.

We decided that we simply must live in a *finca*, and we found a perfect one in the village of San José, which nestles at the foot of the highest mountain on the island, the Atalaya. Our *finca*, which was called Can Palerm, was a pearl of Ibizenc cubic architecture. Two cubes formed the ground floor and a third formed the second floor, with an open veranda. Against the gleaming white mass of the house the wooden banister of the veranda made an elegant decoration. At the back, in a enclosure, was a thicket of prickly pear. In front, a low whitewashed wall encircled the sunk patio and ran, past our little vineyard, down a slope towards the village.

The view from the house was dazzling. Over the twisted dark shapes of our vines we saw the backs of three giant crosses, representing Golgotha, and the large white church surmounted by a tiny belfry with a single bell. Unlike other churches I had seen, which all had elaborate outer decoration, the Ibizenc churches were absolutely unadorned, closed in on themselves, deaf and mute to the outer world.

The layout of the village, too, was unlike anything I had seen in Russia or Germany. The peasants did not live there but on their bits of land scattered around the countryside. In the village, along its only street, were the priest's house, the cobbler's house, the carpenter's workshop, one general store and four bars. The bars, we were told, were strictly segregated along political lines: one Right socialist, one Left socialist, one Fascist and one middle-of-the-road. Interest in politics was intense and political loyalties strong, so nobody went to the wrong bar.

The peasants reminded me of Siberia. Not since my childhood in Siberia had I met with a race of people so poised, so dignified, so impressive as were our neighbours around San José. In some respects they were of course like peasants everywhere in the world – they could be secretive, suspicious, inscrutable – but they were also gracious, generous and blessed with a lively sense of humour which was all their own. They were also good to look at. They were handsome and bore themselves erect. The men wore corduroy trousers and short jackets, black or mole-grey, and the women wore a traditional costume of stiff long skirts over many petticoats and stiff matching kerchiefs over shoulders and chest, with usually a brighter, smaller kerchief over the head. Matrons wore black and the girls muted colours – mixed greys and light browns. Almost all, men and women alike, spoke only Ibizenc, which is the local variant of Catalan. Very few spoke Spanish.

Of all the bars in San José it was the Can Lorenz that particularly attracted us, and soon we were spending our evenings there. Just inside the entrance the owner Lorenzo was usually to be seen, sitting on a low chair with a guitar on his knees. A lean, handsome man, he was a fine player and singer, of flamenco mostly. He and his 'regulars' were socialists, and he would talk politics by the hour. His plump wife Josefa spoke little, but she radiated a placid, friendly warmth. Sometimes their daughter Catalina would sing traditional Ibizenc songs. A shy girl, she had to be persuaded by her mother to stand in front of the bar counter. There she would sing in a touchingly clear voice, which was almost without expression. Strictly according to custom she stood without movement, her lovely face and slim figure as still as a statue.

It was as idyllic a life as one could imagine. Yet its very perfection brought home to me how imperfect and wrong my own life was. It was time to recognise, at long last, that I had made a mistake. In the early summer of 1934 I left Ibiza and Raoul.

17

MEANWHILE THE BERLIN Mensheviks had also left Germany and had found a new home in Paris. There they were carrying on all their usual activities, notably the publication of the *Socialist Courier*. They had even transported their large library and enormous archives. It was natural for me to turn to my old friends, and Lydia and Fyodr Dan welcomed me with open arms.

Within a month my brother Daniel arrived from Germany – alone, as his marriage had broken down. He had experienced much harassment in Berlin. He had seen many of his young socialist friends arrested, and he himself, as a Jew, had been thrown out of his job. Fortunately he had been offered a job in England. A talented engineer and inventor, he had taken part in the early development of electronics in Germany, and in England he was to make an important contribution to the development of computers.

When Daniel went to England in 1934 he took me with him, and both he and I were to live in England for the rest of our long lives. Within a year of our arrival we were joined by Father, who had been living all those years in Danzig. We three were very happy to be reunited. Sanya of course was not with us, but we knew that she was reasonably well situated in Leningrad. Her husband, the Communist Anton Adasinsky, was secretary of the society of former political prisoners, a position which carried the rare privilege of an apartment. And by now they had a daughter and a son. We could not foresee that within a couple of years their whole existence would be shattered.

In one of Stalin's periodical terror campaigns Anton was arrested and disappeared. Years later Sanya was informed that he had died in a labour camp. After Stalin's death he was posthumously rehabilitated, and later still it was revealed that he had in fact been shot within a few days of his arrest. At the time of the German invasion of the Soviet Union Sanya's daughter Galya, a student at Leningrad University, was evacuated with other students to a town on the Volga. Soon news reached Sanya that for some unknown reason Galya had been arrested. She at once set off to make enquiries on the spot, taking her ten-year-old son with her. On arrival she found lodgings and left the boy there while she tried to establish her daughter's whereabouts. So far from receiving an answer, she herself was arrested. Both Sanya and her daughter spent eleven years in a labour camp. As for the son, Sanya never saw him again.

For us in London the ever-present anxiety was about Mother. From 1929 onwards we had been receiving occasional letters from her, but they were so severely censored that they told us very little. In 1936 the letters ceased completely. A year later Father died – perhaps fortunately, for it spared him from knowing what really happened to Mother. More than half a century was to pass before that story became known in full.

After her arrest in 1927/8 Mother spent three years in solitary confinement in the prison of the old monastery of Suzdal'. In ancient times Russian tsars used to incarcerate unwanted wives and rebellious sons there, and in modern times several socialists are known to have been kept there, Martov's youngest brother among them. The cell in which Mother was lodged was in a damp, dark part of the building.

Next Mother was exiled to Central Asia, first to the large town of Tashkent, then to a remote village in the high mountains. In both places she had much difficulty in finding accommodation: at times all she could find was a corner of a room shared with others. To find a job was even harder, as exiles were banned from most occupations. Allowances were doled out, but they were so meagre that they hardly covered the rent, let alone food and clothes. Fortunately Mother still had her sewing skills, and dressmaking and repairs kept her going, badly paid though it was.

In Tashkent there were at least other exiles, people whom Mother could meet from time to time and who helped one another, however hard life was for all of them; but out in the mountains she was quite alone. Moreover, her health had been undermined by her experiences in prison and in transit, and the great changes in climate damaged it further. She developed a heart condition and various other illnesses, and of course there was no medicine available for any of them.

One of the worst trials was the daily trudge to the police station, where exiles had to register.

For some years Mother was allowed to write to, and receive letters from, Father, Danya, myself and Sanya in Leningrad. She wrote that she lived from one of our letters to the next. We also sent parcels from London, but that was a complicated and very expensive business, and usually only half the contents ever reached her. While in Suzdal' she was allowed to receive just one visit, from Sanya. The only detailed information we ever received about her life came from Sanya after that visit.

In 1930 there was an unusually long interval between Mother's letters – and she offered no explanation for that when she resumed writing. It was only much later and from other sources that we discovered the reason for that silence. Mother had been taken to Moscow for interrogation. Throughout 1930 the authorities were preparing a show-trial of Mensheviks, and for that purpose were assembling, from their various places of exile, all the prominent Mensheviks who were still in Russia. As always in show-trials, the accused were supposed to confess to crimes that they had never committed and to denigrate themselves and the party or group to which they belonged. To get committed socialists to take part in such a farce required a long and patient breaking of their moral fibre by intimidation and torture.

For the regime it was all-important to get well-known names in the dock, so several prominent Mensheviks were taken to the inner section of the central political prison in Moscow, the Lubyanka. They included two of Martov's brothers and Mother. But when the 'Menshevik trial' took place almost a year later, in 1931, the list of the accused did not contain those names, which meant that those individuals could not be broken. The accused were either second-rankers or people who had long ago left the party.

After the Second World War there were rumours that the leading figures of all oppositional parties had been shot, on Stalin's orders, at the time of the German invasion. Precise information became available only with the fall of the Soviet regime and the opening of the Soviet archives. Then it was revealed that Mother had been tried by a military tribunal in 1940 and sentenced to death; then retried and sentenced to fifteen years in the prison of Orel; and, finally, tried for a third time and again sentenced to death.

She was shot on 14 September 1941.

Envoi

As, in my ninety-first year, I bring this book to a close, I am very aware how remote the world it deals with must seem. There can surely be very few still alive who knew Siberian exile under the Tsar, or who lived through the Russian Revolution as a member of a family of revolutionaries. Those who can remember what life was like in Moscow and St Petersburg during the Civil War cannot be very numerous either. Even the Berlin and Paris of the 1920s now seem very far away. In fact, the experiences described here belong to the furthermost reaches of living memory. All the more reason for recording them while there is still time.

Bibliographical Note

In the early 1900s my father produced a booklet entitled
My Escape from Siberia, which was published in London by a
press called Free Russia. Before she returned to Russia in
1927 my mother completed her memoirs and arranged for
them to be translated from Russian into German. They were
published in Berlin under the title *Wetterleuchten der Revolution*
(trans. Nina Rubinstein) by a social-democratic book club
called the Bücherkreis. A year earlier, when the author was
already imprisoned at Suzdal', a pirated and much abridged
version appeared in Moscow. Almost forty years later I came
upon the original Russian manuscript at the Hoover
Institution of Stanford University and translated it into
English. This translation was published by the Oxford
University Press in 1967, under the title *Memoirs of a
Revolutionary*. Around 1930 I produced an account, in

German, of my life up to my departure from Russia at the age of twelve. This was published in 1933, under the title *Russische Kindheit*, by Eugen Prager (Vienna and Leipzig). In writing the present volume I have drawn on all these works. The fate of the Mensheviks under Bolshevism is the subject of my book *Lenin and the Mensheviks* (Gower/Maurice Temple Smith, 1987). The 'Menshevik Trial' of 1931 is considered in detail in Appendix II of that work.